The First 100 Years

Best wishes
Z. L. Tesar-Kiszkan
2015

God Bless!
Thank you

The First 100 Years

My family, my life, my joys and my sorrows

An autobiography by
Zdenka Lillian Tesar-Kiszkan

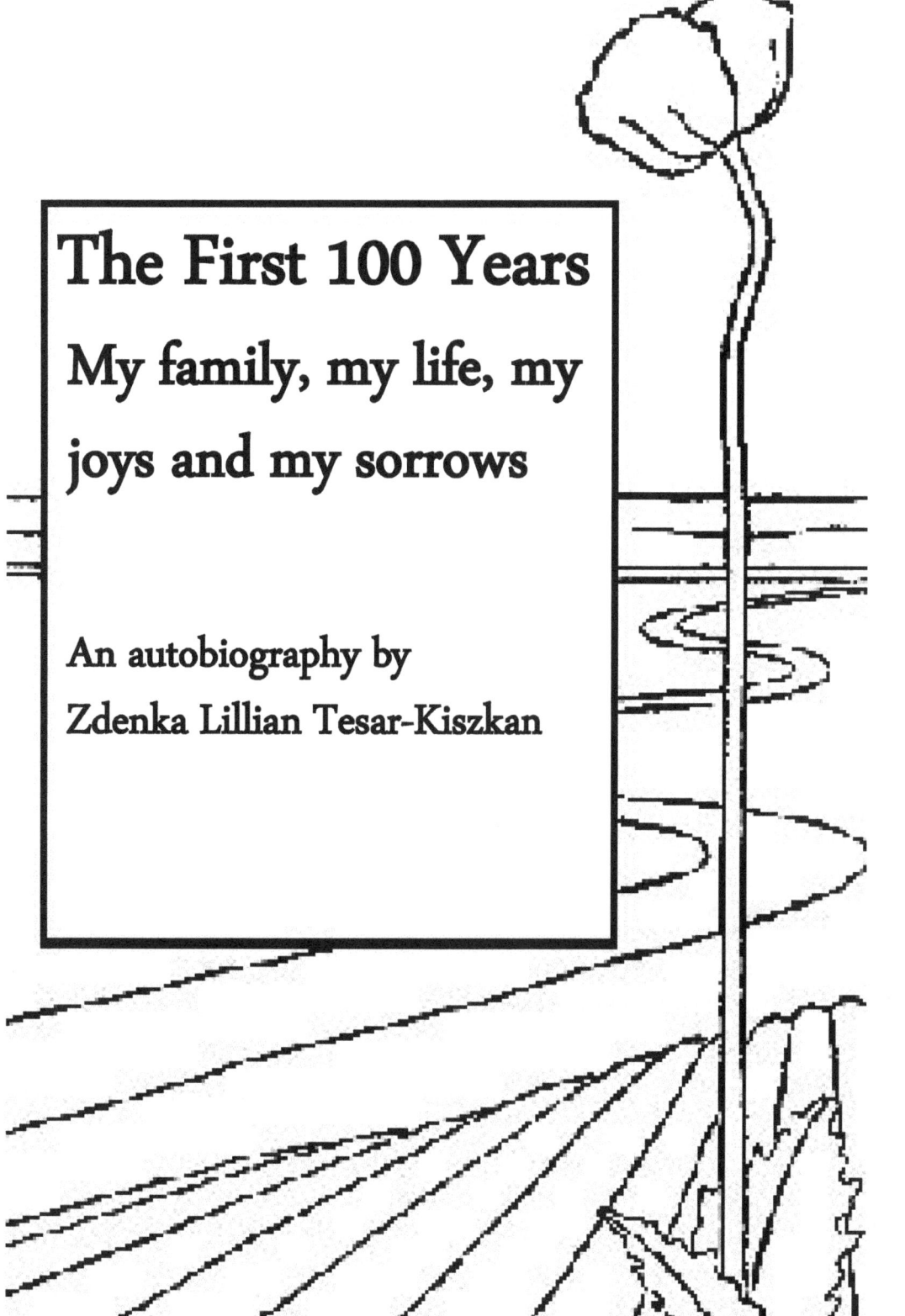

Copyright ©2015 by Lulu author; Zdenka Lillian Tesar-Kiszkan

All rights reserved

Printed in the United States of America

No portion of this book may be reproduced in any form without written permission of the author.

ISBN-13: 978-1-329-01368-1

Prologue

It is said that there are a million stories in the world, yet each is unique, important, and interesting in its own way. So, I hope you will find my story.

It was initially because of the encouragement of my son, John, my other family members and my friends who knew bits and pieces of my life and that of my parents, that I began this undertaking.

There are no words of gratitude that I can express to my daughter, Gloria, my editor, who invested uncountable hours of deciphering, editing, and researching to make this book a reality.

Finally, it is my sincere wish that some of these events will be a source of understanding that life is precious, that all of us are pilgrims on Earth, and that our lives should leave some legacy for future generations.

-Zee

PART ONE:
My father

Jan Tesař

    My father Jan (John) Tesař was born in a little village named Malinky in southern Moravia (now part of the Czech Republic) on September 13, 1883. He was the oldest of four children born to Frantiska [Chmelar] and Vaclav Tesař. He had a brother, Emil, a younger brother, Wilhem, who was born on February 28, 1895, and a sister named Cecilia

Frantiska [Chmelar] and Vaclav Tesař.

    While I do not have a lot of information on my father's siblings, there is one family story about Cecelia. As an adult she married and had had a baby girl. The baby was constipated, and Cecelia's mother recommended giving her a little sauerkraut juice. As the story goes, the sauerkraut juice worked too well, and the baby died as a result. But, back to my father.

In his early teens, Jan was sent to Vienna, Austria to learn the shoemaker trade. To "pay" for the learning from the master, he helped the wife with household chores and watch the children, etc. when he was not busy in the shop. He was given a place to sleep in the corner of the kitchen on a bed of straw. Food was scarce with the extra mouth to feed. Father remembers, and not too fondly, that breakfast at the household consisted often of garlic potato soup with a slice of rye bread. While in Vienna, Jan joined *Sokol*TYRS in Wien, Austria. *Sokol* is a gymnastic organization, founded 1862 by Miroslav Tyrs and Jindrich Fugner, and *sokol* is the Slavic word for falcon. He was then 15 years old.

In the year 1898, when he was 16 years old, my father joined *Sokol* in Brno, Morava (Moravia). He joined as an instructor of the *Dorostenek*(the young women's group).

Jan Tesař is to the left of the girls who are in costume for an exhibition.

Eventually Jan returned to his hometown of Malinky where he started a new Sokol gymnastic organization.. He always believed in the Sokol motto, "Healthy mind in a healthy body." All was not well however, as Jan struggled with the fact that his beloved homeland had been under the yoke of the Austrian -Hungarian Empire since 1816 under the Habsburg family..There had been one revolt by the Czechs and Slovaks in1867, but they were ruthlessly put down and the two former countries lost all of their governmental privileges. Jan, being young and rebellious, staged a demonstration against the Empire by marching thru the village with his friends carrying a coffin draped with the Austria-Hungary flag. Of course, by that evening, there was an order for his arrest!

Somehow Jan escaped and records show that he arrived in New York, NY, USA on April 4.1906 on a ship named SS Christiana, the "mother "ship of SS Resolute.

Ship records

Name:	**Johann Tesař**
Arrival Date:	27 Apr 1906
Birth Date:	abt 1883
Age:	23
Gender:	Male
Ethnicity/Nationality:	German
Port of Departure:	Hamburg
Port of Arrival:	New York, New York
Ship Name:	SS Christiana

His first job was washing dishes in a restaurant and of course *Delnicky Sokol* in New York City gained a member and an instructor for seven years to about 40-50 students. Also in New York, he worked at *Sokol Jonas* for two years where he had eighth grade students. He also bought shares for the *Sokol Delnicky* building. His passion was exercising with wooden bowling pins which he taught the young women class.

One of his highlights during this time was the performance of Diva Emma Destinova, the leading soprano in the Czech opera The Bartered Bride at the New York Metropolitan Opera, on February 19, 1909. On her insistence, she had the *Delnicky Sokol* gymnasts of New York perform as the village crowd in the opera. They sang and danced and all in the Czech language! Dad often talked about this event; he was so proud! He even showed my sister and me the steps of dances he performed and taught the group! The glint in his eyes was a sight to behold!

He moved to Chicago by 1910 as evidenced by the 1910 Federal Census records.

Name:	**John Tesař**
Age in 1910:	26
Birth Year:	abt 1884
Birthplace:	Austria
Home in 1910:	Chicago Ward 10, Cook, Illinois
Race:	White
Gender:	Male
Immigration Year:	1905
Relation to Head of House:	Boarder
Marital Status:	Single
Father's Birthplace:	Austria
Mother's Birthplace:	Austria

He became a naturalized citizen of the United States on April 24, 1915.

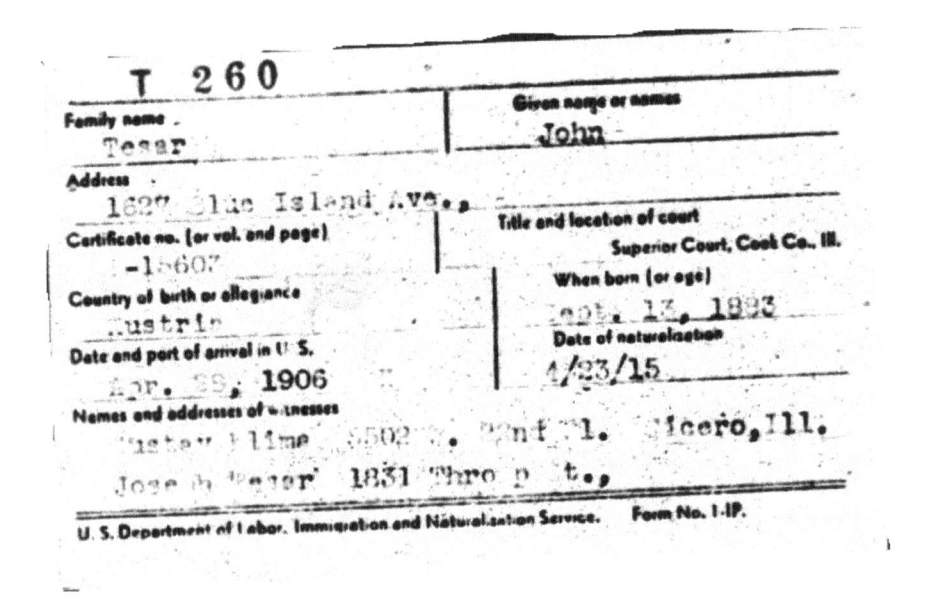

Jan never gave up on his quest to fight for his homeland independence. During World War I, he had an opportunity to enroll with a group of Czechoslovak volunteers in the French Legion which started on August 21, 1914. He officially reported to the service on November 9, 1917. Thus, he became a French Legionnaire and wore his uniform proudly. His armada numbers # 22 were on his uniform collar. An autonomous

Czechoslovak army was established on December 19, 1917 by decree of the French government. On January 12, 1918, the 21st Czechoslovak Rifle Regiment was formed in the town of Cognac, France. It fought as part of the French 53rd Infantry Division. On May 20. 1918 the 22nd Czechoslovak Rifle Regiment was created (Jan Tesař) initially fighting as part of the French 134th Infantry Division. The 21st and 22nd Rifle Regiment saw combat near Vouziers. Jan and his fellow soldiers, endured trenches, but the vision of freedom kept them going till they finally won the struggle.

Jan Tesař in France

On June 29,1918, the government of France officially acknowledged the right of Czech and Slovaks to independence, and the next day both regiments took an oath of allegiance in presence of the French president Poincare as well as Czechoslovak independence movement officials, including Edward Benes. The new country, Czechoslovakia, was made up of Bohemia, Moravia, Slovakia, Ukraine and Silesia. The first president of this new country was Tomas Garigue Masaryk, who bravely fought in France for the independence of the new Czechoslovakia Republic. As the principal founding father of Czechoslovakia, Masaryk is regarded similar to the way George Washington is regarded in the United States. Even to this day, Czechs and Slovaks alike regard him as the symbol of democracy. He took for his middle name "Garigue" which was his wife, Charlotte's, maiden name, whom he met in USA. When I first learned this in school I thought to myself, "What an honor."Mrs. Masaryk was born in Brooklyn in a Protestant family with French Huguenots among their ancestors.

My father was discharged on December 31, 1919 in France. He received the official document of his service crediting him with six years and six months (?) from November 1, 1917 to December 31, 1919. On Jan's 1921 passport application, he indicates that he was in France from August 1918 to February 1920.

After, I recall that whenever my father had the opportunity to wear his French Foreign Legion uniform, as during the parades thru the town of Korycany to commemorate the Independence of Czechoslovakia, he did not hesitate to don the uniform. He also knew the Anthem of France, Marseilles, and was able to sing it with gusto in French!

My father returned to USA and to Chicago .He became a member and an instructor of *Sokol* Chicago. In 1920- 1921 *Sokol* Town of Lake and *Sokol Slavoj*.

Ship manifest 1920

New York, Passenger Lists, 1820-1957 about John Tesař

Name:	**John Tesař**
Arrival Date:	4 Mar 1920
Birth Date:	abt 1884
Birth Location:	Bohemia, Czechoslovakia
Birth Location	Prague
Age:	36
Gender:	Male
Place of Origin:	Tchecoslovauque
Port of Departure:	Havre
Port of Arrival:	New York, New York
Ship Name:	La Touraine

La Touraine

While he was living in Chicago, I assumed that he worked somewhere, but he never talked about where. I know that he had learned, maybe he attended some school, how to MAKE shoes, especially orthopedic shoes for people with special needs. Also, in Chicago, he frequently attended lectures. Specifically I know that he attended lectures at the University of Chicago on Shakespeare and lectures by Dr. Clark about healthy eating and living. He also loved the Planetarium and learning about the universe, etc.

He applied for another passport in 1921. On the application, he lists his occupation as "gym instructor" and his purpose for returning to Czechoslovakia is to visit his mother.

1921 Passport Application

[FORM FOR NATURALIZED CITIZEN.]

UNITED STATES OF AMERICA,
STATE OF Illinois,
COUNTY OF Cook ss:

I, John Tesar, a NATURALIZED AND LOYAL CITIZEN OF THE UNITED STATES, hereby apply to the Department of State, at Washington, for a passport to Czecho Slovakia, France, Germany, etc.

I solemnly swear that I was born at Malinky, Czechoslovakia on September 13, 1882; that my father, Václav Tesar, was born in Czecho Slovakia and is now residing at cemetery; that I emigrated to the United States, sailing from Hamburg about 1906; that I resided 12 years, uninterruptedly, in the United States, from 1906 to 1918 at New York & Chicago; that I was naturalized as a citizen of the United States before the Chief Richard J McGrath Court of Superior at Cook Co. on April 23, 1915, as shown by the Certificate of Naturalization presented herewith; that I am the IDENTICAL PERSON described in said Certificate; that I have resided outside the United States since my naturalization at the following places for the following periods: France, from August 1918 to Feb. 1920,

and that I am domiciled in the United States, my permanent residence being at Chicago, in the State of Ill., where I follow the occupation of gymn. instructor. My last passport was obtained from (army volunteer) on _____ and was _____ I am about to go abroad temporarily, and intend to return to the United States within one year with the purpose of residing and performing the duties of citizenship therein; and I desire a passport for use in visiting the countries hereinafter named for the following purpose: Czecho Slovakia — mother & relations, France & neutral countries —

I intend to leave the United States from the port of New York, sailing on board the _____ on March or April 1921.

OATH OF ALLEGIANCE.

Further, I do solemnly swear that I will support and defend the Constitution of the United States against all enemies, foreign and domestic; that I will bear true faith and allegiance to the same; and that I take this obligation freely, without any mental reservation or purpose of evasion: So help me God.

John Tesar

Sworn to before me this 14 day of Jan. 1921

JAN 18 1921

5961

Clerk of the U.S. District Court, Chicago.

It was on the visit from August 1921 to November 1922 that he met my mother, Beata Tabery in Korycany, Morava (Czechoslovakia) while visiting with his friend. She was performing in a hometown theater, which was quite a common entertainment during the winter time. Other clubs and organizations held dances, Masquerade Balls, concerts, etc. My father's friend, Frantisek Blecha, knew my mother and offered to introduce my father to her. After they met, Father was captivated by her and felt that he finally had met the girl of his dreams. This was the woman that would become mother of his children. The one problem was that he had to persuade her to leave her family and join him in USA. Not an easy task.

New York, Passenger Lists, 1820-1957 about John Tesař

Name:	**John Tesař**
Arrival Date:	25 Nov 1922
Birth Date:	abt 1885
Age:	37
Gender:	Male
Port of Departure:	Bremen
Port of Arrival:	New York, New York
Ship Name:	George Washington

The George Washington

Back in Chicago, Jan was active in 1922 Sokol Rozvoj and in 1923 Sokol Lyons and Sokol Slovan,

> *Denní Hlasatel* -- January 08, 1922
> ## The Sokol Hall in Lyons The Sokol Slovan Will Celebrate the Opening of its Own Hall
>
> This day will be a memorable one for the small Czech colony of Lyons, for it will celebrate the opening of its own Sokol Hall. This accomplishment was possible only after a great many sacrifices....Lyons, which formerly served as a picnic ground for our Chicago countrymen, today boasts of a goodly number of Czechs who live here. For some time now they have also had a Sokol association. It is this association which has so tirelessly worked toward the establishing of its own home, and its efforts have finally been crowned with success.....
>
> The Hall is located on Gage Street, and the celebration attending the formal opening will be held there. It will start at three o'clock in the afternoon. The program will include gymnastic, musical, and dance numbers. After two musical renditions on the program, the building will be officially declared open by the building committee. This will be followed by gymnastic exercises by girls and women, and several interesting dance numbers. It will end with the playing of the Bohemian and American national anthems.
>
> The evening program will start at 7:30 with a brisk one-act play in which members of the association will take part. The evening's entertainment will close with a dance.....

Jan was instrumental in Sokol Delanski Yugoslavian and, later, Sokol Liberec for about 4 months. He participated in many Sokol exhibitions and took part in IX Sokol Slet (Czech word for flocking of the birds). This gathering of Sokol athletes, resembles the Olympic Games with competitions and callisthenic exhibitions. These were quite impressive, since many of the Sokol units gathered from all over Czechoslovakia and performed in unison.

PART TWO:
My mother

Beata Tabery

Time out for Mother. Beata Tabery was born on February 18. 1896 in the little village of Brankovice in southern Moravia to Anna Vanova (Vana).

Anna was the oldest child of thirteen and was born in 1870. Anna's parents were Josef Vana, born in1840 and Johanna nee Radvanovska (Radvan). When Anna was of age, there was not any employment to be had in her village, so she was send to the capital city of Brno where she was employed by the family of a military commander. She cooked for the family, cleaned and did other chores. The commander often entertained his officers, and one day a handsome officer, Julius Tabery, so dashing in his uniform and sporting an elegant mustache, was a guest in the home. He was the conductor of a military orchestra and was in Brno probably to discuss some concert or band performance sponsored by his commander. The country was under the Habsburg rulers at that time, the Austria-Hungary Empire with Franz Josef the Emperor. Julius must have been smitten by Anna's looks, and his visits to the home became more frequent. Sometime later, on one of his visits, there was no Anna! His commander told him that Anna had just vanished! She did not leave any note of explanation for her departure. They did not know her home address, and so it took some time to locate her.

Julius Tabery

Julius finally did find Anna, and then it took several months for him to be released from his obligation in military. At that time, when men signed up for military service, it was for a long time. I also think that, maybe, Julius had planned on making a career out of the military. After being released, he immediately traveled to village of Brankovice, Moravia. What a tearful reunion that must have been! He also found out that Anna was carrying his child! Anna was always considered the level-headed one; everyone looked up to her. It had been a hard decision for her to return home in her condition, but she did not have any other choice. There were 13 children in the family and some of her sisters gave birth to children without the benefit of marriage. It still took some time for the wedding and Beata was born. By this time, my mother always told us that her mom, Anna, said that little Beata was dancing at their wedding! This seems to me not to be true, since Beata would have been only about 10 months old. Well, she might have been an early "walker"! The name Beata (means "blessed") is a German name, and Julius was the one who named her. To me, it sounds like he felt he was blessed by her birth.

Why was she given a German name? Well, the story goes that Julius's grandfather fought with the French army in Russia with Napoleon Bonaparte in 1812. After their disastrous defeat when Napoleon conquered Moscow and found the city deserted and burning. There was no food, and the French army was freezing, ill-equipped for the cold. Napoleon had no choice but to retreat. His troops were dying from the severe cold temperatures and hunger and they endured attacks by the Russian Cossacks. Out of the 600,000 Napoleon forces, all but 27,000 died or had deserted. During their march back to France, Julius's grandfather reached the center in Europe and settled in the town of Horni Roudna, which is in the southern part of Germany (that later became later part of the country of Czechoslovakia). There he married and raised his family. Since I was not able to locate the town on any map, my suspicion is that it either "died" or was annexed or merged with another town. This explains why the language Julius spoke was German.

A slightly older Julius Tabery

Julius, his grandson, (my mother's father and husband of Anna) was born in 1870 to Jan (Johann) Tabery and Viktoria Dvorak. I do not know if my grandfather had any siblings, but mother mentioned that as a child, once a year or so, he took her to visit his family in Horni Roudna. They rode on a train, which confirms that there was quite a distance between the towns of Korycany and Horni Roudna.

After Anna and Julius' marriage, my grandfather, being out of the military, was now without a job and therefore without an income to support his family. He took a job as a gardener, keeping the grounds of castle Lednice in southern Moravia.

The first historical mention of this castle was in 1222, in which the Czech king, Vaclav (Wenceslas) I, granted the castle and land to Austrian nobleman, Siegfried Sirotek. At the end of the 13th century, the Australian Lichtenstein family became the owners of the whole Castle Lednice and surroundings. The castle had been redecorated many times, and when my grandparents worked there, it had the only functional hothouse in the European continent. It housed many exotic plants trying to mimic the Garden of Eden!

So this is the place, where my grandmother, Anna, became the cook for the family of Prince Lichtenstein living there at that time. My grandfather Julius, was employed as a gardener, keeping the grounds and working in the conservatory. The Duke and Duchess of Lichtenstein had a young son, and soon little Beata and he became playmates. They had the freedom to run outside and inside the castle. Mother told me that once, as they were running thru the halls, the boy knocked down a huge Oriental vase that was standing in one of the halls, and it crashed to the floor in thousands of pieces. I wonder who was more scared, Beata or the little boy? Of course when it came to reckoning and offering explanations, she ended up as the guilty one! Bad news, the little boy of course blamed little Beata for breaking the vase!

Lednice Castle today

An opportunity for Julius came when the Thonet factory in the nearby town of Korycany began hiring local people. In 1856, Michael Thonet opened up the new factory there. He was the founder of an establishment, the Gebruder Thonet. He was awarded a bronze medal for his Vienna bentwood chairs at the World's Fair in London, 1851. In 1855 he was awarded the silver medal as he continued to improve his production methods. The town of Korycany was best suited to him because of the abundance of beech woods that surrounded it. His 1859 chair, Nr.14, better known as Koncumstuhl Nr.14 (coffee shop chair no14) is still the "chair of chairs" with some 50 million produced up until 1930. It yielded Thonet a gold medal at the 1867 Paris World's Fair. These chairs were sent all over the world.

Koncumstuhl Nr.14

The owners of the Thornet factory came from Vienna, Austria, and they built a mansion near the factory and spent summers there. It was a grand building with well-cared grounds which were enclosed by ornamental iron fence. They even had a tennis court! No one was allowed in there. My uncle, Julius (Jr), told us that the new factory was forming an orchestra and were looking for experienced musicians to form a band. Well, my grandfather qualified, after all, was he not a musician in the Military? So he was employed as a varnish finisher with an opportunity to play again in the orchestra! I was told that he also played at dances in town.

Lhotka Street where the Taberys lived in Korycany

When Beata was out of school, her mother Anna sent her to her sister Justine Hanko in Vienna, Austria to be the house helper. The Hankos owned a butcher shop where they both worked. They needed someone to take care of their daughter, Mitzi, walk her to school, pick her up after school, and watch her until the family returned home. She also cleaned the apartment and did the cooking for the family. She recalled that when the couple returned home in the evening, her uncle brought the bloody butcher aprons to be scrubbed which became part of the Beata's chores. That was one job she really detested!

Beata and friends circa 1915 She is standing on the left.

Mitzi, to the left, is the girl that Beata cared for. The woman on the right is Beata's Aunt Justine, sister to Beata's mother, Anna.

Justine Hanko had another daughter that was adopted by another of Justine and Anna's sisters, Cecelia, (remember there were 13 siblings in this family) in Korycany, since her and her husband were childless.

In 1905, a son was born to Anna and Julius, and they named him Julius, what else? Beata was then 9 years old. When young Julius was still a young child their father, Julius Sr., died in 1917. Family legend says "he blew his lungs from playing the wind instrument!' Beata now felt that it was on her shoulders to make sure that her brother finished school and learned a trade. She therefore quit school and became the sole breadwinner in the family working in the new Tomas-Mundus furniture factory in the shipping department. The workers, mostly women, would wrap the furniture in straw. Those days, mothers stayed home with their young children. There was no Social Security for widows or government financial help. Beata had to support the family and pay the mortgage on their cottage. She worked in the packaging department, and, during lunch hour, Beata would run all the way home! The factory was on one end of the town and their home was on the other. I think this was to check on her mother and her little brother.

The family raised chickens and rabbits; they had a goat and raised a pig every year. To preserve the pork meat, they stored it in salt brine and had some smoked at the local butcher. While Beata was at work, young Julius and Anna went looking for firewood. Their only heat was the kitchen stove. They also had a vegetable garden and grandmother did a lot of canning, I am sure. In the back of their house was a little stream "Kyjovka" where Julius would fish. He had to be careful though because he was really poaching. Those were hard times, and no one seemed to complain; they all shared the same situation.

There was a Chateau/ castle overlooking the town which was owned by royalty, the Wittgensteins from Vienna. It was their habit in the summer months to come to stay at their chateau summer place. The large park surrounding the Chateau was available to anyone when the owners were not there, and many of the town's people enjoyed walking through it on Sunday afternoons. The large lane that led to the park was lined with huge chestnut trees and it was a favorite "lovers lane" for young people. Of course, when the owners were visiting, the grounds were closed to the public. The town's people liked their royalty, and they entertained them with plays on the balcony of the chateau. Mom recalls that the school often had the children put on little skits and sing songs to the delight of the royal audience. The Wittgensteins owned several acres of land in the surrounding area, and they hired local workes to cultivate it. They owned stables with horses available to them to ride in their park. There was also some wild game there for them to hunt in the wooded park surrounding the chateau.

Then a new attraction came to town: a movie house! Black and white silent movies! What a novelty! Money was short, but all the women in the packing department wanted to go and see the movies! Beata was selected to go and see the movie. The ladies all chipped in and purchased the ticket. Afterwards, Mother told them all about the movie, scene by scene, and all of the ladies were spellbound! She had a captive audience. Of course, mother was now a young lady and there was no shortage of young men showing interest in her. Mother had a special friend who was a schoolteacher, an important position in town, and, after several dates, they decided to marry. But this was not to be, because he died of tuberculosis.

When mother's brother, Julius, was finished with school, he needed to learn a trade to be able to support himself. As was the custom, he was taken in by a local tailor to learn the trade. There were no trade schools then. By the early 1920's, he had finished his apprenticeship and was able to earn his living. He left for city of Prague to seek an employment as a tailor. He became established at a prestige custom tailor shop as a pattern cutter.

It was about this time that my father, Jan Tesař, appeared on the horizon. He was on one of his home visiting trips from USA, visiting his mother. He attended a local theater production with his friend, Frank Blecha, as was the custom of entertainment during the winter months. Father shown an interest in one of the young actresses, Beata. Luckily, so it seemed, Frank knew her and offered to introduce them. So they met and most likely dated a few times before my father had to go back to USA.

Frank's wife, Teresa, was Beata's best friend. They worked together at the Thonet Mundus furniture factory. They stayed friends for life. Frank and Teresa always treated me as a second daughter. They lost five of their seven children to the 1918-1920 Spanish Flu pandemic. The two remaining were Karl and Anna. Anna then died as a young woman from a dental infection. Teresa struggled greatly with her grief. Fortunately, her son, Karl, lived to a ripe old age. The last time that I saw Frank and Teresa was in 1949 while I was visiting the Czech Republic.

Jan writes on his 1924 passport application that his purpose for the visit was to visit family and get married.

1924 Passport Application

PART THREE:
My family in America

Beata, Jan, and Family

After my father arrived back in Chicago, Illinois, where he lived with two other bachelors in an apartment (he was a bachelor himself at 42 years), he could not get Beata out of his mind. He decided to write to her and enclosed a steamship ticket for her to come to USA to join him AND to be his wife! Her reply was, "If you want to marry me, come and get me!" which he did and they married in May 1925 in the town of Kyjov (the county seat) at a Court House in a civil ceremony.

When my dad, the long-time bachelor, went to Czechoslovakia to marry my mom, he suddenly acquired cold feet and did not show up for the wedding! How embarrassing for Mother! She had to swallow her pride and return to work and not too happily, I am sure. One month later, Dad showed up with apologies. Of course mother forgave him, and they got married and embarked on their trip to USA.

It was with a heavy heart, that Beata left her mother, but since her brother, Julius, was on his way to adulthood at the age of 18 with a tailor's trade, her mother gave her blessing for Beata to leave. She must have seen the trip as a great adventure with an uncertain future in a new country and with a new husband. After taking the 5-day long steamship trip to New York, the newlyweds took a train to Chicago. Mother remembered an incident on this train ride. She was hungry, and when a porter came through the train offering sandwiches for sale, Father bought her one. When he saw that it was made with white bread, which according my father, was un-healthy, he threw the 2 slices of bread out of the window and mother was left with just the meat! I am sure that did not satisfy her hunger much!

Here is the ship manifest showing their arrival back in America in 1925. There is no record of Beata.

New York, Passenger Lists, 1820-1957 about Jan Tesař

Name:	**Jan Tesař**
Arrival Date:	29 May 1925
Birth Date:	abt 1884
Age:	41
Gender:	Male
Port of Departure:	Hamburg, Germany
Port of Arrival:	New York, New York
Ship Name:	Resolute

S.S. Resolute

On the ship, there were many passengers and many acquaintances were made. My parents struck up a conversation with a man named Hynek Selucky. He came from the neighboring village of Bukovany and his occupation was a shoemaker! He was going to Texas to help his uncle on his ranch. My parents and he exchanged addresses.

Jan and Beata settled in Chicago in the Pilsen neighborhood in an apartment that father shared with two other bachelors. This was not to my mother's liking, so after two weeks of my mother's scrubbing the walls, windows, washing curtains, etc., father found a shoemaker shop with living quarters behind the shop. This was on Kedzie Avenue and 51st Street. Mother helped him in the shop, polishing shoes and waiting on customers. She remembered that people would drop off their shoes needing repairs on their way to the movies, and would pick them up as they were returning home. Later, during the depression, repairing old shoes instead of buying new ones was common and business was good.

THE OLD PLACE
2615 W. 51st St.
SHOE REPAIRING SHOP

Is for your family the best.   The lowest prices in the neighborhood
POLISHES - LACES - BRUSHES - STRAPS
If we please you — tell others   If we don't — tell us

JAN TESAŘ, Mgr.

This was an advertising blotter for my father's shop. We lived in an apartment behind.

After the first month of marriage, my mother was not pregnant which baffled Father. Another month went by and still there was no pregnancy. After three months, father was wondering if mother would ever be able to bear children! After all, their ages were catching up with them. Mother was 13 years younger than my father which made her 30 years old! Finally, after their fourth month of marriage, Mother was pregnant.

I was their first child and was born on June 22.1926. Father was very concerned about the pain accompanying the birth process and hired Dr. Molner, who came to the house for the child delivery, to give mom a pain killing injection at a cost of $50. Such an expensive procedure was unheard of in those days, but father insisted. Zdenka, the new baby girl was named after my father's favorite Czech author, Karel Borovsky's daughter, who had died in infancy. Mother's choice for the baby's middle name was Lillian, after the heroine of a book mother was reading at that time.

Mom, Dad, me at 2 years old, and our car

About this time, my parents received a letter from Hynek Selucky, the shoemaker on his way to Texas that they had met on the S. S. Resolute. His uncle had died and the family had no interest in the ranch. It was up for sale. This meant he was becoming home-less and penniless. It was not possible for him to return to Czechoslovakia, and he was asking my parents for help. Of course my father invited him to Chicago, and he stayed with my family for some time. Even though they had a child (me) they found a room in their home. Father then helped to find him a shoemaker shop and loaned him the money to get himself established.

My parents' second child, another girl, arrived on August 12. 1929. They named her Miroslava, loosely translated as "one that celebrates peace." I believe now, that she was named after another of my father's hero. Miroslav Tyrs, co-founder of the gymnastic organization of *SOKOL*.

The landlord family lived in the upstairs apartment. They had two young boys, who became our playmates. Mom remembers that almost every morning she served for breakfast shredded wheat in a bowl of warm milk with an extra cup of milk on side. And almost every morning, I knocked over the cup of milk! This was because I was watching the boys already playing in the yard and wanted to hurry to join them!

The landlord kept some chickens in the yard that ran freely. Of course, their droppings also dropped freely! One day, I really do not remember this, Mother caught me munching on something. When she questioned me and was digging in my mouth, she discovered that I had found a new snack. Yup! Chicken poop! Sorry, but I can't tell you how it tasted!

Our life was quiet. We often visited Father's friends on Sundays, and he attended meetings the Free-thinkers. He called them his church! I remember that he had an uncle or some sort of relation, living in Chicago at 2432 South Homan Avenue His name was Frank Zizlavsky. More about him and the house will follow later.

2432 S. Homan

This house became very important to my family. One memory stayed with me until my old age. It was on returning from one of these visits. All I remember is that it was a rainy night. As we arrived at our house, I do not remember if we came by a tram or if father had his Chevy, we began to cross the street. I was eager to get on the other side. I heard my father calling out to me to wait, but I was clutching a special gift and was eager to get it into the house. Later I found out that it was some kind of a statue that I received on the visit. Paying no attention to father's warning, I started to run across. As I looked to my left, all I saw was the darkness and cars head lights and the rain! I had the thought, "I AM IN TROUBLE! Should I turn back, should I speed up, or should I just stand there and hope the cars would stop?" Mind you, I never dropped the statue! I don't remember if I made it across the street or if father got to me before I did, but that was one scary moment. It must have been for father also, as he retold the story later.

Another story that Father told me was about a time that he was babysitting me. He gave mother an evening out once every week to attend the movie theater in the neighborhood. On Wednesdays, there were giving FREE dishes to the patrons! Well at home, everything was going well until I decided that I wanted something. I kept saying "tatashee, tatashee." Poor Father kept going through the apartment, pointing to different items, but I just kept on with the "tatashee." Finally, I grabbed his nose and pulled on it! I wanted a "handkerchief!" So much for Father's babysitting!

The house we lived in was across from the Crane Company. I believe they made plumbing supplies. The factory had a lot of empty space surrounding it which was fenced in, but still gave me a feeling of living in the country, almost. It had a very tall clock tower that was for visible miles around. Many people set their clocks and watches by it. It also chimed the hours.

The Crane Company

When I was four years old, my parents enrolled me in kindergarten at the Marquette Park School. Each day, Mother walked me there and also picked me up. I do not remember much of my time spent there except for one incident. I was leaving the school to wait for mother. I remember the wide stairs leading to the main entry doors. There were many children rushing out of the school, and one of the boys knocked me down. I remember laying on the steps bleeding from my lips with a teacher bending over me. I felt the loving comfort of that teacher assuring me that everything would be OK, Mother was on her way! And she was, and I survived.

Our family, of course, belonged to the Sokol organization, which became our social life As a matter of fact, I was even baptized at Sokol! My godparents were Mr. and Mrs. Frank Vorel, also members of Sokol. We attended many of the Sokol functions and after my father bought a car (I do not know the year or make, I think it could have been a Chevy), we traveled in summers to the Sokol Camp in New Buffalo, Michigan (By the way, the car was stolen just before we made our move to Czechoslovakia. My father's comment was: "Oh, it was the Mafia").

1930 United States Federal Census about John Tesař

Name:	**John Tesař**
Gender:	Male
Birth Year:	abt 1884
Birthplace:	Czechoslovakia
Race:	White
Home in 1930:	Chicago, Cook, Illinois
Marital Status:	Married
Immigration Year:	1906
Spouse's Name:	Beata Tesař
Father's Birthplace:	Czechoslovakia
Mother's Birthplace:	Czechoslovakia

Household Members:	Name	Age
	John Tesař	46
	Beata Tesař	34
	Zdenka Tesař	3
	Miroslav Tesař	0
	Julius Tabery	25

Sokol event in Chicago. Jan Tesař is in the back row 4th from the left. Julius is 5th from the left.

Julius is the man on the bar.   Soldiers Field 1930   Zdenka and Mirka 1931

    In the above picture, my mother was taking a picture of us to send home to my grandmother in Czechoslovakia. She insisted that I keep my little sister sitting in the chair. I remember my frustration in this almost impossible task!

1935 Cousins Jarka and Martha Navratil

These were my mother's cousin Elizabeth's (Betty) daughters.

By now, even though the new family and business were going well, Mother started to miss her mother, Anna Tabery, and brother, Julius Tabery, left behind in Czechoslovakia. Father also left some siblings and his mother. His mother, Frantiska, was living with her son, Emil, in the town of Slavkov or, in German, Austerlitz (This was the site of the famous Battle of Austerlitz, where Napoleon effectively crushed the Russian-Austrian army in 1805). Emil and Frances had no children. She was a retired home economics teacher. My uncle had a stroke some time before and was paralyzed on his left side. My aunt's mother also lived with them, so the two older ladies were companions to each other. Father came to realize, that none of their families, especially my grandmothers, would ever know his children born in United States. So they started to think of returning to Czechoslovakia and building a home in Korycany. This was the little town where my mother's family had their home.

So it was decided, that mother and father would build a house. My mother's mother, Anna Tabery, was able to secure a lot in the small town of Korycany where she lived. I seem to remember that there was an old house on the property that had to be torn down. My father had an architect draw plans in Chicago and mailed them to the builder. Plans were being made to make the move back to Czechoslovakia when the house became ready. Since the town of Korycany was a recreation area, surrounded by the Chriby Forest, Father hoped to find renters eager to live there.

Passport photo. Left to right: Miroslava, Zdenka, and Jan Tesař

      It took quite a long time for the house to be built. The local builder was commissioned to use the plans that father had mailed to him. It was a challenge. Not very many homes in this little town had indoor plumbing. The well had to be drilled, but it was a problem deciding how to store the water that was to be used throughout the entire house. They finally decided to install the holding tank in the attic. In order to hold this huge tank, the floor in the attic was made with bricks to hold the weight. Water then was pumped from the well in the back yard using electricity to turn the wheel on the pump to get the water into the tank. Quite a feat! But it worked! They also planned an enclosed back porch with a tiled floor. It would have an attached pantry on one end and a bathroom with a tub on the other end.

PART FOUR:
My family in Czechoslovakia

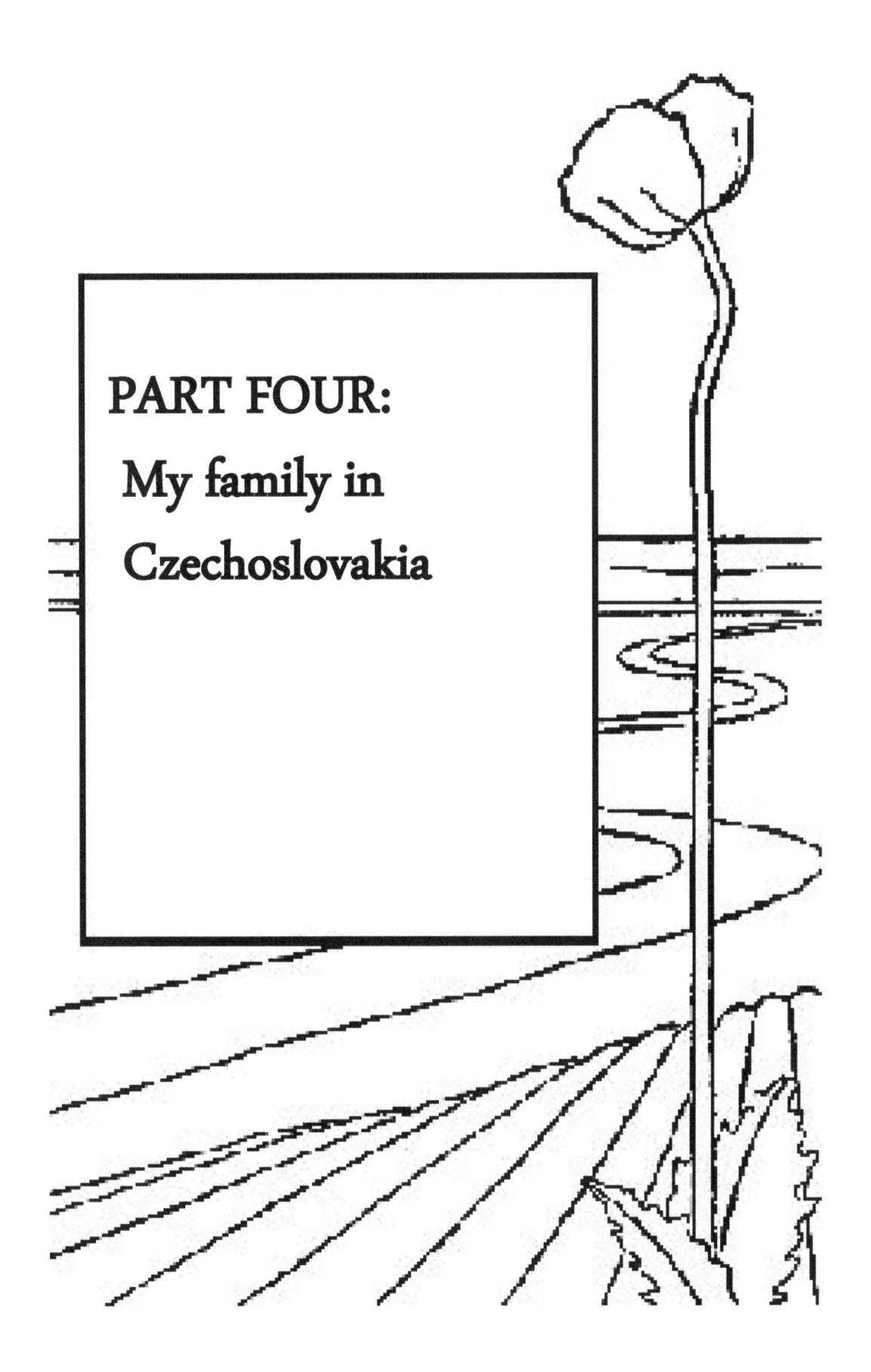

After the new house in Korycany was built in 1931, it was time to arrange our departure. I do not have the name of the ship, but in August we were on our way! By this time, I was five years old and my sister Mirka (short for Miroslava) was 2 years old. While we were on the ship, my sister celebrated her 2nd birthday on August 12. The captain of the ship presented her with a fruit basket and, on urging of my mother, I walked around the deck offering fruit to the children traveling with their families. One other moment I remember is when we were all seated at long tables having dinner. The overhead lights were swinging, and they were just bare bulbs hanging from electric cords. I imagine, the swinging was caused by the ship rocking from side to side. The dessert was a square of red Jello, and I remember the jello shaking on my plate. Why that stayed in my mind, heaven only knows. Other than these two memories I do not remember the rest of the trip.

Anna Tabery (Vana) She died in 1944.

In Korycany, my mother's mother, Anna Tabery was already settled in our new home She would be living with us. My first impression of the house was really no impression at all. My sister and I were more interested in the beautiful decoration that Grandmother had made for us. In the hallway there was fresh moss on the window sill, decorated with marzipan little mushrooms! We were so impressed and fascinated by it. Of course, later, we discovered that the marzipan mushrooms were EDIBLE!!

My father's sister, Aunt Cecelia, came to visit soon after our arrival. I cannot remember her face. I only recall that she had a large brimmed black hat, and that she was bending over to kiss my little sister. That is the only time that I saw her.

These are my Grandma Anna's sisters. I believe the sister on the left is Anastasia. Cecelia is on the right. Cecelia married Rudolf who died in 1956.

Cecelia adopted Marie, who was her sister Justine's baby. Marie is shown below as a child and as an adult. She died at age 18.

    Our new home was a two story building with a marble staircase leading to the second floor. We had parquet floors in the living room and bedrooms. Mother also purchased a Persian carpet for the living room and smaller carpets for the bedrooms. On the second floor, there were 6 large rooms that could be made into apartments. There were built-in stoves in two of the rooms to accommodate kitchens. There was also a large balcony the width of the building. The first floor, where our apartment was located, consisted of a kitchen, two bedrooms, a living room, an additional covered veranda with a tiled floor bathroom, and a pantry .One bedroom was for my mother and father. It had two single beds, pushed together with nightstands by each of the beds and two armoires, one for linen and the other for hanging clothes. Above their bed, was a large print picture in a golden frame. The scene was captivating and I spent much time looking at it. There was a beautiful water nymph queen resting in an ornate boat and being pushed by other nymphs onto the lake. Such a serene, beautiful fairy tale tableau. Stairs led down to the formal grassy yard with a flower garden. In our living room, there was a fireplace with an extension into the adjoining bedroom. The fireplace was made with imported Italian green marble. One bedroom had a tall tiled heating stove for warming the room in the winter. There was no central heating! From the kitchen we could enter the store, which later became the shoe and leather store.

The kitchen had a built-in white tiled stove for cooking and heating and a sink for washing dishes In the middle of the kitchen was a big round table where the family gathered for meals. My sister and I played a lot under that table. I remember one day, my sister started to cry because she could not see! I was blamed that I had done something terrible to her! This created a commotion in the house until mother discovered that she had been chewing a piece of gum and had put the chewed gum over her eyes! Another time, my little sister was rummaging through some drawers when Mother discovered that she had her hand clenched. Mom insisted that she open her hand, but she kept on squeezing her fist more and more till blood started to trickle down her wrist. A razor blade had severed her middle finger! The doctor was able to put the finger together, but her finger was crooked from that time forward.

We also had running water throughout the building. So we had flushing toilets and a hot water tank in the bathroom which was heated with wood for baths.There was also a big garden where we raised some vegetables, some potatoes, and hay for the animals. We had two goats to milk and, later, three goats so we always had milk. Mother made sour cream when she let the milk sit in the pantry. We churned our own butter in a hand operated churn. Because goat milk is white, grandma grated some carrots, put them in a little cloth and squeeze the juice into the churn, so the butter would have a yellow color.

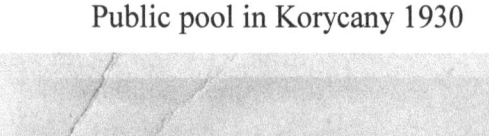

Public pool in Korycany 1930

After father got us all settled in, several months later, he returned to USA for two more years, to earn more money for the new house. During the time that Father was in Chicago, he was able to attend The Chicago World's Fair, The Century of Progress International Exposition in 1933. I remember him bringing us souvenirs, playing cards and some little cards with pictures of the exhibits. I believe I still have some of those cards. I even have a poster of the event.

OFFICIAL POSTER FOR 1933 WORLD'S FAIR

The official poster for Chicago's 1933 World's Fair beckons the word to come and see her Century of Progress Exposition. She is the Miss Chicago the world has known since the famous World's Fair of 1893. The familiar Phoenix on her head blazons the city's motto, "I Will." The Indian head in the background recalls the Chicago of 1833, a little village in the Red Man's wilderness. A bold white checkmark against the dark map of the United States will serve to remind America — and the world — that Chicago will be the Mecca of tourists during the Exposition.

Two years later, my father returned from USA to Czechoslovakia. From the US, he brought large sacks of green coffee beans and 5 or 6 Philco radios. The local grocery store would roast the coffee beans for us as needed. To save on the coffee beans, our coffee was grounded daily in the coffee mill hanging on the wall near the stove and we added roasted wheat kernels and chicory for a dark color. There was a chicory factory in town. As you can surmise, Dad was a health conscious man and many a time for breakfast he would cook a pot of whole wheat. He was way ahead of his time, with all the emphasis on whole grain health benefits nowadays.

After my father's return, he started the shoe and leather goods store which was already built at our new home. I remember his trips to different shoe factories to pick out shoes to be shipped to our store and also the salesmen bringing samples of ladies' shoes for mother to choose from. We added stockings and belts, purses, wallets to the store inventory and the business took off. Later, I remember that father priced the goods as he knew was done in USA, for example 9.99 KCS, not quite 10.00 KCS! It was a new idea for the town's people. And they all had a good laugh!

Father also loved the big garden and planted about fifty different fruit trees: apricots, peaches, and cherries, mostly dwarf trees, an English walnut tree and a hazelnut. The whole garden was lined with red currant bushes from which we made wine. I remember one summer, one of my father's beloved peach tree seemed to be withering. After much examination, he discovered a wormhole in the trunk of the tree. So he got a wire, heated it red hot, and forced the wire upward through the hole, until he successfully killed the worm and the tree was saved! Oh how happy he was!

Down the center of the garden was a path and that was lined with black currant trees and gooseberry trees. Dad also built us girls a little cement swimming pool. However, it did not have a drain so the water was not very good for swimming. It was rather small, probably about 6' by 10'.

There was a huge pear tree in the middle of the garden that I loved to climb. I remember one time that I climbed to the very top of this tree. While enjoying the view of the garden below and the neighborhood, I heard Mother calling my name walking through the garden. Hmm, I guess I have done something wrong and climbing the tree was my way escaping punishment! I kept quiet until sometime later when my sister appeared looking for me! Well, I decided that if she were looking for me and not my mother I should climb down! I do not remember if I was punished! Another time, Father found a used tire and made a swing which he hung on the pear tree. My sister had a bit of a problem to use the letter R, it always came out as an L One day as she was swinging, suddenly, the letter R came rolling from her lips! She kept on swinging and singing RRRRRRR! We were all so happy for her!

So a new life began for all of us. I remember the Sunday afternoon visits of my grandmother's sister Cecelia Kocarik who lived in our town with her husband, the grandmas with their *"babushkas"* (head scarfs) on their head (sometimes special *babushkas* imported fromTurkey) having their afternoon coffee and visiting. Some Sunday afternoons, Mother dressed us girls up, and we went for a walk thru the town.

At one time in our house, there was a dentist office with two waiting rooms and an apartment for the family, plus another two room apartment rented by a Seven Day Adventist preacher. She held Sabbath services on Saturdays in her living room which became the church. She invited us to attend, and we asked our friends to attend also. What did we know? It made her happy and it was fun anyway. It was there I heard some of the first stories from the Bible. I was still very confused with Moses and Jesus. Could not understand WHY Moses was renamed JESUS later on in the Bible!

I remember one summer, I decided to put on play. The space under our upstairs back porch was open with columns supporting the upstairs, a perfect stage. I wrote the play, and my sister and I had the leading roles with one or two extra "actors." We also needed scenery so we went to the near forest and cut down some small pine trees to decorate our stage. I do not remember what the play was all about, but I do remember that our parents had a long lasting laugh at our performance. Especially the famous proclamation of my sister saying, "Ha, the queen lieth here, dead!" We also had an audience and charged them each a penny! Well, halers, which are similar to pennies. Or was it 5 halers, after all, it was a "big" original production with props!

My father had also a gazebo built for us girls and furnished it with wicker furniture. No one in town had that! One night I decided to sleep in there. I guess I was not brave enough, because in the morning I found myself in the house in my bed!! How did I ever get there it is still a mystery! I must have walked in my sleep! Probably scared, but of course, I would not admit it!

My father would make us girls high winter boots. For the upper part he used heavy blankets that he quilted and finished with a leather portion of the lower shoe. Yes, we were the ONLY ones that sported these! I remember when my sister and I were small, we might have been, about eight and five years old, Dad made us new shoes. They were summer shoes, beige, with a strap across the top, fastened by a little button. Well, by this time, we girls wanted store bought shoes, not homemade shoes! The first time we were going to wear them was on a Sunday afternoon for the traditional outing thru town. Mother got us both dressed and we were to wait outside, in front of the house. It was a LONG wait. I think, to amuse ourselves, we were inventing games to play. One of these "games" was to drag my sister behind me, which successfully scraped the toes of her shoes. Of course now, she was not able to wear her new shoes, lucky for her, but it did little for me! All I got was a spanking and the "privilege" to wear my new, homemade shoes!!! My sister was the winner!

I was to start kindergarten in the town, even though I had already attended one year of kindergarten in Chicago.

The hardest thing for me was speaking in the Czech language all the time! I felt very timid. When we lived in the United States we communicated in Czech at home but, with friends, I had conversed in English. So I was bilingual. The thing I liked the best though in the new kindergarten was playing with clay, creating little animals and people. That helped my transition into the new environment. We did not wear uniforms, but we all worn aprons over our dresses to keep them from getting dirty. Mine was made from special material, rough to touch, but shiny. We wore these throughout the school years all the way to eighth grade.

The school started on the 1st of September, and the first day of school was the most dreaded one. All the first graders got inoculated by the local doctorDr. Tomasek. One by one we marched to the teacher's desk to receive our inoculation for small pox. The doctor came back weeks later to inspect if the scratch inoculation "took." We learned our cursive alphabet, math, and reading, and when we reached the third grade, we learned how to knit mittens and later how to knit gloves using four needles for knitting the fingers! In the higher grades we learned how to mend socks and sew an infant gown and cap by hand. Later, we used sewing machines to make an apron. And in eighth grade, we learned how to cook and sew a night gown! We learned embroidery also. I loved to draw and paint, we used mostly water colors. For our first art project in the 5th grade, we were to bring a flower to use as a prop to color. Well, that was right down my alley!! I was absorbed in my painting of a yellow dahlia, when the teacher stopped at my desk. He picked up my painting to show everyone in the class, "that is what he wanted!"

First grade. Zdenka is in the last row on the right end (standing).

When I was about five years old, I remember that I had to have a tooth pulled. I courageously walked to the office (I do not remember the procedure), but I cried loudly all the way home because I had a hole in my mouth.

Miroslava is on the left of the first row. Zdenka in in the third row center. This was at one of the *Sokol* outdoor exhibitions

I remember the school activities, end of the school year outings, puppet productions, and *Sokol* gymnastics performances, the Sunday walks to the nearby forest, the sledding in winter, and ice skating on the town's pond. I remember the celebrations of holidays, sometimes national holidays with parades thru town in the evening and children carrying lanterns to light the way. I remember the harvest festivals when we dressed in our national costumes, the celebration of young men going into the army, the *Sokol* gymnastic exhibitions outdoors (in the winter they were held indoors). During the outdoor *Sokol verejne cviceni* (exhibits) in the field, we were awarded the traditional *parek* (hot dog) and *rohlik* (bun) which was so special! As we got older, we were introduced into social life at the special dances held during winter. The dance held on New Year's Eve (St.Sylvester) was attended by the entire family, and it was always an event to look forward to.

6th grade. Zdenka is in the first row, second from the left with her arms folded.

Did I mention that I was a publisher and an editor? In 8th grade I handwrote a 4-page newspaper with news about the school. It also featured a serialized novel, which encouraged my readers to purchase the next issue to see what the next sequel would bring. The charge to read my publication was about 5 cents. I only published one copy of each edition, and the students had to take turns reading it.

It was fun when Uncle Julius, Mom's brother, came to spend his summer vacation with us. He always brought with him many, many socks for mother to wash. I have never seen so many dirty black socks at one time! I thought he must pretty rich to own such a great wealth of socks!

In the summer, it was time to pick currant berries for Mother to make wine. The making of the plum whiskey came later, as we gathered the fallen fruit and stored it in a barrel. During fall months, the town had a distillery, and the citizens were allowed to distill this potent whiskey. Harvest time! It was a time of preparing for the winter.

When we were sick, mother's remedy was to give us a warm cup of wine spiced with cinnamon stick and to make us rest in bed to "sweat it out." Winter was never boring. There were dances sponsored by the Social Democrats, the Sokol gymnastics club, the Orel Catholic gymnastics, the Young Peoples' Club concerts by the town's choral group, and such. There were sponsored dances, formal dances, theater plays, masquerade balls, a New Year's Eve dance (St. Sylvester Day). We had a movie theater in town which was open on weekends, also skiing in the mountains on trails, and ice skating on the local pond. Some very industrious young man erected a shanty on the pond and sold hot tea, flavored with rum. Hey, it was cold out there!

Zdenka's first traditional Moravian costume

On one of the sledding outings in the forest, Father came with us and piled a bunch of us kids on one sled. Not good! The sled overturned and my little sister ended up with a broken arm! She was at the bottom of a pile of several children, no wonder!

Christmas season started with visit from St. Nicholas on December 6th. St. Nicholas would go house to house through the town. He was a person dressed as a bishop and accompanied by an angel and a devil. We children really dreaded this, because he "knew" all about our mischief (compliments of our parents), and there was no chance to hide or to lie! Also we had to recite our prayers, but since we did not go to church, we were in trouble already! The angel held a golden book containing our deeds and misdeeds where it was all recorded. The devil would be rattling his chains, ready to haul us to his domain if we did not promise to change our "evil" ways! In the morning, we were rewarded with little gifts from St. Nicholas that he left on our window sills! There were cookies, oranges, candy, and nuts. Sometimes our treats were on the kitchen table the following morning! According to the legend, St Nicholas and his crew descended from heaven on golden ropes. Talk about my imagination, I swore that I saw them doing this! But mother just laughed, and said I must have been dreaming it! So much for my visual documentation.

During the Christmas season, we were always cleaning the house to get ready for Christmas Eve. There were cookies to be baked (and hide away from us children). There were many legends and customs that happened on Christmas Eve. For instance, all animals talked that night! Sorry to say, but I never heard them. No matter how much I wanted to stay up and be in the goat barn, it never happened! Probably because I fell asleep! One of the best things that happened every Christmas was Uncle Julius would come home! This meant presents, always a book or two and some jewelry. He was a bachelor, but I guess he still knew what little girls wanted. My sister and I were secretly searching to buy presents for Mom. I don't remember buying anything for Dad or Grandma and Uncle Julius. I still have the "golden" rose broach that we gave mom one Christmas!

Here are my sister and I ready for a Sunday afternoon walk with mother wearing our brand new coats with fur collars.

Our Christmas tree always had chocolate foiled treats. They were sold in sets at the stores. We also baked special cookies to decorate the tree. When we were little, we would never see the decorated Christmas tree until Christmas Eve when it was all set up gloriously shinning with burning candles in the living room. It just took our breath away seeing all this beauty! During that day, we were not allowed to go in that room.

One Christmas Eve, we heard a lot of noise, Grandmother gathered us and hid us in her bedroom. Something mysterious was happening! There were sounds of bells which could only mean that Baby Jesus was making His rounds delivering presents! Wow! Of course we could not see Him, because that was forbidden! As we sat huddled together in the bedroom with our hearts pounding, what a wondrous sight I saw! Grandmother's bedroom had a large window that was opened to the covered porch. There was a reflection of my father carrying precariously a wonderful decorated Christmas tree! Well, I thought to myself, he must be helping Baby Jesus decorate the tree and now he is just carrying it inside! Never-the-less, it was quite confusing to my little mind! And then, as grandmother ushered us out of the bedroom and into the kitchen, we saw Mother coming out of the hallway. Of course we excitedly reported to her that she missed Baby Jesus who just was here! The kitchen door was wide open! She questioned Grandmother, "WHY do we have the door open?" Oh, such tales to tell to the unsuspecting, innocent children!

Carp is the traditional fish used for the Christmas Eve Dinner. These carps are specially raised in ponds for the holidays. After mother purchased our fish, it had to be kept alive until that evening. The fish was put in the bathtub and we had a chance to play with it chasing it from one end of the tub to the other! No baths for us! This kept us busy, because if we fasted that day, we were supposed to see a golden pig image on the wall! Well, another thing that never happened to me! When it was time to prepare the fish and cut it up in chunks for frying, we watched the pieces quiver as mother was salting them. Amazing sight! We also begged for the fish's air bags, still full of air. We learned so much about the anatomy of animals from the farmers' ways.

After the first star appeared in the night sky, it was time to sit down and eat supper. We had to make sure that there were even number of guests around the table. If not, someone might be missing next year, most likely by death. I remember one Christmas, when my father was in the Concentration Labor Work camp, mother had me go and fetch a child from one of our neighbors to even the count. The supper meal started with fish soup which was made with the head of the carp. Then, vegetables and farina-breaded pork cutlets, potato salad, fried fish, dried fruit compote, cookies and the traditional braided sweet bread, Vanocka, also called Houska.

Another custom on Christmas Eve was to gather all the crumbs from the table and carry them to the orchard to scatter around the fruit trees to assure a good harvest. Some of the tidbits were to be given to the house dogs and cats. Another custom for single girls was to go in the back yard and shake a tree, listening from which direction a dog was heard barking. From there, your future husband would come! Also tossing a shoe, while standing with your back to the door. If the shoe ended pointing toward the door, you would be leaving the house that year, if not, you were destined to stay. We also cut apples, crosswise, to see if we will be healthy in the coming year, If the star that was formed by the seeds in the middle of the apple was clear and without a blemish, your health would be good. If not, well you needed to prepare for illness. Another custom was floating half empty walnut shells with little candles in them in a large bowl If your shell floated across the surface to the other side of the bowl, you might be going on a sea journey in the coming year! No cheating by blowing on the shells to "help" them float!

My father's brother, Emil Tesař before his stroke and his wife, Frantiska. Emil died in 1952 while we were in the US. My aunt then went to live in Brno near her sister. The smaller photo is an older Aunt Frantiska.

On Christmas Eve evening carolers went from house to house singing carols and carrying a small manger. They were rewarded with small change and Christmas goodies. There was a midnight service at the local church. I did go one time, and it was so peaceful walking thru the town with snow falling and covering the sidewalks. The full moon shone so bright, it could have been a re-creation of the first Christmas Eve so long ago. I enjoyed the service, especially the singing of the choir. One of my best friends, a schoolmate, sang a soprano solo. Beautiful! By the way, as I am writing these memories in 2013, she is still singing at the age of 87! On Christmas Day, we visited our friends' homes to admire their trees and to have some of their goodies from the tree. We also listened for the cracking of a whip by the local shepherd going thru the village. He was the one who took care of the farm animals in the summer months in the pasture outside the village .Every morning, these farm animals were let out of the farmyards and joined the ones gathered already walking through the village. The shepherd returned them later in the afternoon for another feeding and milking. On Christmas Eve, the farmers rewarded the shepherd with some extra cash and, of course, goodies.

On Epiphany Sunday, the Three Wise Men walked from house to house to bless the house and marked the door post with the initials, KMB, for Kaspar, Melchior and Baltazar, the names of the Wise Men that visited the Christ Child.

Then the winter set in. This was the time when the women gathered in houses to strip the goose feathers that they had gathered throughout the year. These were to be used in pillows and feather quilts. There were usually 5-6 women. No sneezing or coughing was allowed or feathers would blow all over the room! It was a time to catch up on local news and gossip, and exchange recipes, etc. This took several evenings and the end was celebrated with a home cooked dinner and some cordials. Then the group moved on to another house.

Family portrait
Miroslava is seated on her mother's lap and Zdenka is on the table. 1932.

Winter months were also used to butcher the family pig. This was a big event! On the designated day, the local butcher came to our house and the pig was hauled out of the pen and butchered. The poor pig squealed so loudly, that we girls locked ourselves in the farthest room away from the yard. We even hid under the covers, so as not to hear the poor pig cry! The butchered pig was then cleaned in a trough filled with hot water and lye, and using chains under him, cleaned of all his hair. Then he was strung up and cut up by the butcher. In the meantime, the intestines had to be scrubbed, by turning them inside out, and rubbing them on the side of a wooden bucket with some salt and lye. These were used for making sausages by filling them with cooked meat. Some of the larger ones were filled with blood and barley and cooked in a large kettle In order to preserve the meat, some was taken to local butcher to be smoked, some was put in salt brine, and the rest was canned. The lard was rendered the next day, and that took all day. There were no freezers to be had. We shared some of the products from the hog with neighbors, who in turn, shared some of theirs, when they butchered their pig. We kids usually delivered these to them.

When Easter was approaching, another cleaning of the house was in order. This was a time for painting, repairing and so forth. Before Easter Sunday, every corner needed to be thoroughly swept and cleaned with no cobwebs left behind. It was a beginning of another season.Spring was on its way! Time to get rid of the old winter. Some of the villages had a custom of carrying out the old winter witch. This was a small tree without leaves, decorated with strips of linen and topped with a "head" made with straw.

Easter celebration in our house, was mainly the Easter Sunday meal. By this time one of our goat's kids was ready to be butchered. I think we had a goat for Easter because it was similar to a lamb. Of course we did color eggs; we had plenty of those. We used natural dyes: green from cooked spinach, yellow from onion skins, and red from red beets. We had some very talented old grandmas in the village that decorated special eggs. First the eggs were dyed deep purple, I believe they used the purple indelible pencils for this (horrors by today's standards) and then they used a special scratching hand tool to scratch intricate designs on the eggs. These were very special and treasured for years.

Did you know that a Good Friday holds a special magic? If you picked a certain herb on that day, it could heal anything! Also all of the church's bells left their churches and flew to Rome to return back on Easter! The Resurrection of Christ was celebrated on Saturday evening! I remember sneaking into the church during the Holy Week to see the body (statue) of Christ displayed in a tomb. It was mind boggling to me. Every time I went by the church, I went in. I do not know what I expected to find, but it was all so mysterious.

More fun was to be had on the Monday that followed Easter Sunday. The custom was to get rid of all the stale winter dust, even from ladies! This morning was dreaded by all women, young and old. Sometimes, with the help of mother of the house, a bedroom wondow was conveniently left open so that the young men could catch the young girls unaware, sometimes still in bed! They were whipped with a special switch, made by weaving pliable willow twigs.. It was an art in itself. There were several of them, very skillfully braided together. The boys were hiding around corners to catch the young girls as they were going to church on Sunday. This was to be a warning, what they should expect on Easter Monday. I remember one Easter, some of our parents' male friends surprised mother and she really got whipped, until she was sore! It was all supposed to be in fun. Some fun. At least it was not a dunking in a barrel of liquid manure as was done in some other parts of the country. Can you believe, that these boys and men were expecting some rewards?

The first of May was a special day. One of the customs was erecting a Maypole in secret by a young man in his special girl's back yard. It was an evergreen tree, decorated with paper ribbons affixed to a tall pole. Sadly to say, it only happened to me once, and I never found out who the boy was.

In May, the local Catholic Church celebrated a feast. There were altars set up all around the town's square, decorated with flowers. The priest walked from one altar to another, and school children, all dressed up in their finest outfits, followed him. They dropped flower petals as they walked. I joined them once I did not really know what was going on, but all my friends were there and I wanted to wear my pretty dress!

The family grave in Korycany

Summer brought weddings, and those were fun. The custom was that the mother of the bride did not attend the wedding church ceremony. Of course the groom came to the church alone, but before he could enter the church, he had to BUY his entry! Older women would string a rope across the doors. They offered him a "bride," a women figure all covered in veils, but, when he declined, he had to pay them off! Usually the "bride" was unveiled and it turned out to be one of the old women from the village! Lucky for the groom! Of course, there was laughter!

Back to more serious things: school. The obligatory school system consisted of 8 years of elementary classes plus and extra 1 year which was voluntary. After that, students were able to take a test to qualify to attend an eight year gymnasium comprised of four years of high school and four years of higher learning. At this last level, students could choose a college of their special interest. The elementary school started at 8:00 a.m. and I was always late. Well, almost always. At noon, there was a break for lunch, then classes resumed from 1:30 until 3:30 p.m. Several girls walked to school some distance from neighboring villages and were allowed to stay for lunch at school, the rest of us went home. There were separate schools for girls and boys.

At the end of my 8th grade year which was the year many would graduate, our class was planning a puppet show for the younger classes. I remember I had the role of the witch in Snow White, but I got sick. It turned out that I had either scarlet fever or diphtheria.

As it was, when I went to the hospital, the whole house had to be disinfected, even the piano keys. I do not think my sister minded that! The night, going to the hospital was another adventure. When the doctor came to the house, he had me strip off my bed clothes and very gingerly, trying not to touch me, made me turn around to inspect all those red dots on my body. He decided that I needed hospitalization. Since we did not a have a car, mother had to hire a taxi to drive me several kilometers to a hospital. I still have a hard time believing that she sent a young sick girl to the hospital alone with a strange taxi driver. To make things worse, the car had a flat tire in the middle of a wooded area. It was raining and the driver had to fix it in the dark and in that rain while I sat in the taxi feverish with a scarlet fever rash! The puppet show was postponed in hopes that I would recover, however I was quarantined for six weeks in the hospital, and the school puppet show had to go on without me!

I spent three weeks lying in bed and a no protein diet for another three weeks. Because I did not walk the first three weeks, my legs were weak and I had to learn to walk again! I also suffered from arthritis. The doctors said it was a side effect of the scarlet fever. When I was first admitted, I was put in the Diphtheria department. I guess it must have looked pretty bad. After taking a culture of my throat doctors decided I should be in the Scarlet fever department. Either way, both were contagious, so I was allowed no visitors for the entire six weeks. Mother came, but I was only able to visit with her from the hospital window! I spent the first three weeks in bed, but did not mind. I spent my time drawing. The nurses brought me paper, pencils, watercolor paints and brushes. I was happy. I especially loved to draw Snow White and Seven Dwarfs. This was my favorite American movie which I had seen at our movie house. I also liked to paint sunsets, because I loved the colors. After returning home, I spent some time at Aunt Teresa's (my mother's friend) and Uncle Frank's home. Mother wanted to make sure I was no longer contagious to affect my sister.

We visited special historical places in our woods such as the remnants of the stone stairs of the pulpit, from which the St. Methodius and Cyril, preached. They were monks that were sent from Rome to the Slavic nation. They were the ones that created the written Slavic alphabet, called the Cyrilic alphabet.

We also climbed the ruins of the castle Cimburk whose owners owned the countryside in past. There is a legend, that when the castle Cimburk was being attacked, there was an effort to save the wooden statue of Mary with the Infant Jesus in her arms. A farmer hitched horses to the wagon and retrieved the statue from the castle's chapel. While driving away, he wanted the horses go faster and used the whip. While doing so, he accidently swished the whip across the face of Mary in the back of the wagon! To this day, it is said that scar is still visible on the statue that is now in the town's Church.

Cimburk Castle ruins

There are a lot of pre-historic sites and many archeological digs around the whole countryside; it has been inhabited for many centuries.

PART FIVE:
The War

While I was busy with my childhood endeavors, my peaceful existence was being threatened. The Sudetenland, located on the Czechoslovakia border with Germany and Austria, was occupied by Adolf Hitler, the Führer of Nazi Germany, on October 10, 1938. While the Czechs had been prepared to fight, the French and the British were not. British Prime Minister, Nevil Chamberlin, delivered the Sudetenland to Hitler at the Munich Conference. Then, on March 14, 1939, Slovakia seceded to the Germans. The same day Hitler summoned Czech President, Dr. Emil Hacha, to Berlin. **Hitler demanded that the Czech lands be incorporated into the Nazi Reich as a "protectorate". A broken Hacha telephoned Prague and ordered that there should be no resistance. The Wehrmacht crossed the border and occupied Bohemia and Moravia in one day.**

Adolf Hitler established by proclamation from the Prague Castle the Protectorate of Bohemia and Moravia on March 16, 1939.

Adolf Hitler at Prague Castle

Back in my hometown of Koryčany, rules and regulations were established targeting mainly the Jewish population in an effort to separate them from the rest. They were forbidden from participation in any sports, their children could not attend school, they received smaller rations of food, and they had to wear a yellow Star of David on their clothing with the word, Jude (Jew). The schools suffered because all female married teachers were forced to resign and all teachers over the age of 55 were put on pension.

Did I mention our neighbors, Mrs. Stern and her son Kurt? She collected hides of farm animals. When we butchered a rabbit, we children would take it to her and she would pay us some small coins. Once a month or so, someone came and collected all that she had accumulated. They were Jewish and no work was allowed on the Sabbath, so sometimes she would ask us kids to light her stove, because that was considered work.

The Koryčany Jewish cemetery was full of head stones. It was tended carefully and we children used to play there. There was an intriguing small building at the entrance to the cemetery. This was used by the Rabbi to ceremoniously wash his hands signifying that he had nothing to do with the death of the deceased. There was no blood on his hands! The Jews also had a temple in town, and on the Sabbath they held services. We children used imitate the Rabbi's singing if we were passing the synagogue on that day. Then we would run like crazy so as not to get caught!

Jewish Cemetery, Korycany

In the fall on 1941, my parents enrolled me in the voluntary 9th grade. I was 15 years old. This class was held in the boys' school which happened to be next door to our house. Our class was small, compared to the other classes, probably 20-25 students, and it was coed. The algebra was hard, and I had never liked math to begin with. We also had biology, zoology, some chemistry, and simple engineering, but the best class of all was drawing! This class was taught by the principal of the school. Since this class was supposed to prepare us for life, the drawing and painting assignments were geared toward an occupation as were the other classes. So our project in art class was often creating an advertisement for a specific product. We also had homework from this class, and I spent many Sunday afternoons drawing, painting and designing. I also did homework for my classmates at times. How naïve I was, thinking that the teacher would not recognize these that had been drawn by me! By this time, I was designing my own clothes, even coats. Every village would have several seamstresses, and I am sure that our local seamstress, Mrs. Vaculik, cringed when I showed up with my material and my designs!

I liked biology, and one Sunday afternoon the principle of the school saw me in our back yard (the schoolyard and our yard were separated only by a fence). He called to me to come up to the school! There I saw something that I have never forgotten. He kept silk worms in an aquarium, and I was introduced to the process of raw silk!

While I enjoyed these childhood moments, life for many during the Nazi occupation of our country became a life of fear. Many of our own people became our enemies. No one was sure whom we could trust. Life was regulated by new laws. Gone was the freedom of the new Czechoslovak Republic that began in 1918. The Nazis had big armed forces to feed, and the food had to come from somewhere. Our food was rationed. Meat was purchased with food stamps. We were allowed ¼ kg of meat per week per person. So if there were four people in your family, you could get one kg per week, IF the butcher had some. When he did, we had to make sure we had a place in line, before the store opened his shop. Many times I would go and wait in line and when I was nearing the door, Mother would come and take my place. Beef was only available if a cow broke her leg and had to be butchered. Sometimes, we could get horse meat, but we were not fond of that. However, we were allowed to keep rabbits and chicken. Another regulation, only one chicken per family member. If you had more than that, you HAD to give the government 60 eggs per each chicken a year. Sometimes the control went through the town, and, if we knew about it ahead of time, we could gather the extra chickens and hide them under the beds. They kept quiet while in the dark, and we were saved from the control! Sugar was also rationed, but we were able to produce flour and butter ourselves. Also we were able to produce the feed for our animals. We had three goats, so we always had plenty of milk and butter.

Every night we had to cover our windows with black cloth to snuff out any visible light, so the enemy would not detect our town. There were controls over this also. They went on high grounds to make their inspections. If your house had any light oozing out, you were fined and warned! Of course, the radio news covered only the victories of the Nazis, because the radio was controlled by them. The only real news we were able to get was from Radio Free Europe from Great Britain. We huddled nightly at the radio making sure all the doors were locked! We also had a big map of Europe hanging on the kitchen wall, where we followed the advance of the Allied troops.

During this time, the secret Nazi Police came to town. Well, they thought they were secret but, we all knew that they were there. They were on the look-out for anyone who could be a possible suspect of disobedience to the Nazi rules. The teachers were really targeted as were the business people and, of course, the Jews. There were 36 people from my town who were sent to concentration camps. Of these, 9 returned.

After the war was over, one Jewish man, Arnost Kohn, returned to town. He had changed his name to Kadesh (I discovered much later that this was a name of a town in the Old Testament of the Bible). This is the one person that my parents helped out, probably saving his life. He was able to escape before his whole family was taken away, and he ended up in England. Once Arnost was in England, his mother came to my parents hoping they could help him because of their contacts in the United States. My parents transferred $2.000 to Arnost in England from their bank account in Chicago. Mrs. Kohn gave mother some jewelry for collateral. Helping a Jew put my parents into a great jeopardy punishable by death. Another time, Mother recalled, that one day as she went to gather some hay for the animals out of the barn attic, she noticed an impression of a body in the pile of hay. Whose it was, we will never know and no one knew at that time either. Mother kept it to herself.

After completing 9th grade, I was sent to a boarding school in the town of Slavkov or, in German, Austerlitz, in 1941. Because Hitler wanted the youth to be educated, students were spared from being sent to Germany to work in ammunition factories, producing war equipment. That was the reason I was continuing my education.

All of the young people who were not in school listened to the radio once a month to hear if their birthdate and year were to be announced. All those born on that date had to report to the city hall the next day. There, they were told when and where they were going to be shipped to Germany to work in factories that made war materials.

Safely at a boarding school run by Roman Catholic nuns, I was studying to eventually become a home economics teacher. Even though I was not a Catholic, the Mother Superior agreed to take me in, but I had to follow their daily routine! Mother felt that I was safe in that environment. Though it was quite an experience for me! There was the morning silence with a praying nun walking in our bedroom while we washed in individual wash basins by our beds. Our beds were separated with white curtains, for modesty purposes. Then was the chapel visit, mind you, still keeping silence, and only when we went to the dining room for breakfast, were we allowed to talk!

My class at the boarding school. I am seated at the right.

Classes started at 8:00 a.m. in the adjoining building. I liked the classes, because not only we were taught the basic sewing and embroidering, we had to design the edgings of a pillow case and also our initials to be included in creating a custom made article. We also designed specialty table cloths with interesting edging and embroidered designs. Of course I liked the drawings! I must have caught an eye of a nun that was painting altar coverings and priests' garments for I was invited into the cloister quarters to help with painting – mostly bunches of grapes and sheaves of wheat – I loved it! I felt very privileged for NO ONE was ever invited inside the cloister! This made me feel a bit better, for I was always referred to as "the American" almost as a derogatory slang.

Heating fuel was scarce, so our classrooms were cold. We sat in our coats and wore gloves to write. We had no textbooks because of the shortages. Only the teacher had a book, and we wrote down the lessons as she read them to us.

Life was quite structured with prayers, school, and recreation which was walks in the garden. We also had one hour study time in the late afternoon, which was another silent time! However, Saturdays and Sundays were free!

Sometimes on Sundays, I was delegated to ask the Mother Superior if a group of us girls could leave the boarding school to explore the town. At times we had to have a nun to accompany us, but other times, if we were lucky, we could go alone!! Wow! We felt like the birds, FREEE! Of course we had a time limit, but that was OK.

Since I was participating in all the religious routines of the convent, the nuns eventually decided that it was time for me to become "officially" a member of the Catholic faith! They made arrangements with the local church and priest for me to be baptized! Yikes! My mother was never even consulted on this! All I remember is that I was wearing a long white dress, where it came from it is a mystery to me to this day. All of the nuns were present at the church, but I do not even remember the ceremony, if there was one! I named a friend of mother's, Kveta (Flora), to be my godmother. She lived in another town, so she was not even present!

Lidice

While I was safely tucked away at my Catholic boarding school, on May 27th, 1942, Reinhard Heydrich, the Nazi controller of Bohemia and Moravia was attacked by two British-trained freedom fighters – one from Bohemia and the other from Slovakia. A grenade attack on his car left him fatally wounded, and he died soon after. In retaliation, Hitler ordered the destruction of the town of Lidice to "teach the Czechs a final lesson of subservience and humility".

Soon afterwards German troops invaded the small town and rounded up all of the villagers. They were separated into two groups: men and boys over the age of 15 and women with all remaining children. All 173 men were lined up against a wall ten at a time and shot. The 19 men that had been gone at work the day the town had been invaded were gathered later and also shot. The women, who numbered 198, were sent to Ravensbruck concentration camp. There were 98 children and of those a handpicked number was selected for "Germanisation." The majority of the children were gassed. Moreover, the village of Lidice was utterly and completely destroyed. Even after being burned to the ground, it was bombed.

Today there is a memorial where the town used to be. It has a museum with all of the photographs that the Nazis took to document their work. There is also a rose garden with rose bushes sent from all over the world and a huge life-size sculpture of the all the children.

Here are my sister and I in 1942. I am 16, she is 13

My home economics school was closed after one year and taken over by the Nazis who made it into a hospital to take care of their injured soldiers. Of course, the school ceased to exist and I was back home, wondering what to do next! It was the same year, 1942, that my father was arrested and sent to a concentration camp.

The first time he was arrested, according to the archives of the city of Hodonin, was on January 20, 1942 by Agricultural Control for not reporting the full amount of wheat harvested. You see, we grew wheat and were supposed to report how much wheat we harvested each year. Then, our ration of wheat was reduced. Kyjov County had no record about the results of punishment given. I seem to think, that this was done after my father was imprisoned and mother was the one who dealt with this.

The second time he was arrested, according to the prisoner records in Kyjov County, was by the Gestapo on December 28.1942. He was held in Kyjov jail overnight. The next day, December 29, 1942, he was transported to Land Court Prison in Brno (the capitol of Moravia). There he was imprisoned until August 24, 1943, the date of trial. He was arrested for not reporting the complete inventory of shoes in our shoe and leather goods store. There is a bit of a story as to how this came about.

My mother had a second cousin Adolf Jurcicka, whose father had died and lost the family home. He was homeless and my mother asked my father if Adolf could come and live with us to help with chores in the fields to earn his keep. Of course Father said yes. They made him a bedroom behind Dad's shoe repair workshop situated in the formal yard behind the big house. He helped with harvesting and some chores. He took meals with us in our kitchen. One day, he visited the local pub and the men started to ask him questions about our family. They kept the drinks coming his way and soon Adolf spilled his guts. He answered the questions they were asking him and soon they all knew that my father was not loyal to the Nazis. At that time, everything was rationed including the shoes. Each person was issued only 2 pairs of shoes each year. Sandals with wooden soles could be bought without a ration ticket but were not very good for working in the fields (this was a farming community). My father secretly hid shoes and boots at different friends and relatives to keep them from being counted in the store inventory as the Nazi government demanded.

According the trial records in Brno which was held on August 24,1943, my father was accused of not following the Nazi orders by hiding and not reporting the amount of shoes on hand in our shoe store. On his trial transcript, it mentions, one of his "faults" was that he accumulated quite a sum of money while in United States and also became a USA citizen by naturalization .He was accused of wanting to gain profit, according to the lifestyle he had learned while living many years in United States. This was also where he learned these tactics as per their reasoning.

Brno, the town where the trial took place.

Sadly to say, all those people that were so willing to help my father with hiding the shoes were given sentences to serve as their punishments. There were 10 people involved: some were family, some were neighbors, and some were friends who disliked the Nazis as much as the rest. My father's brother, who lived in a nearby town, also kept some leather materials for repairing shoes. He got scared, reported the hidden goods in his keeping, and took them to the police station. Since mother admitted saving some children's and ladies' and men's shoes for her own family, she was not punished because it was meant for immediate family use. Since the Nazis wanted to keep the store operating and Mother having two young daughters, ages 13 and 16, she was allowed to return home.

While my father was imprisoned in Brno, before his trial we were able to visit him once every 6 weeks. The trial ended at 6:15 P.M. August 24, 1943. The special court was held in Uh.Hradiste (town) with a lawyer representing the German court from Brno, Justice Rebeschte residing, lawyer JUDR Gessauner representing my father, Advisor Weiss, the state's representative: Dr. Arkus, and the official Justice secretary Kunster to oversee and record Court proceedings.

The Court's decision for my father's punishment was two years in the house of correction penitentiary institution with hard labor. He would be granted time, of being jailed since Jan 21,1942 to August 24,1943 and, according to the law, also time used for investigation would be counted as part of the sentence to be served.

We had no idea where or when he was going to be transported and mother was frantic. She had a German lawyer who must have been sympathetic to her situation, so he kept a watch on my father's deportation date. One day, she received a notice from the lawyer: Father was going to be shipped to somewhere to Germany on a specific date and would she want to be at the railroad station on that day? Of course, mother made arrangements to be there. She had no idea if she would be able to see him. After some search throughout the railroad station, she found the platform! There were mostly women there shoving and crying, and children hanging onto their mothers' skirts. All were hoping to see their husbands and fathers and say their last goodbyes. The Nazi police were trying to keep some order with the crowd. There were several boxcars that made up the train. The boxcars had small windows near the top about 3-4 inches tall. Father was not a tall man and the possibility that he could get near the window was quite remote. I wonder what was going through the minds of those prisoners. I am sure they were not told of their destination or for how long they would be in the boxcars. The boxcars were filled to capacity. I cannot even estimate how many men were in each box car. Fifty, seventy five, one hundred? They were all standing, supporting each other, leaning on each other. The chaos on the platform was deafening

As the train started to move, there was more wailing and waving. Mother held her white handkerchief which she started to wave, hoping that father would notice! There, there, was that father! Did he see her? She thought that she saw his blue eyes and she thought he saw her. After the train had departed, sadly, she turned to leave the platform and catch a train to take her back home. There was a business that she had to run, fields to be taken care of, and a family to feed. It was a future full of challenges, all without her husband. How would she be able to handle this, alone.

After my father was sentenced and was shipped out of Czechoslovakia, we had no news about his whereabouts and no contact with him whatsoever. Mother kept in touch with the German lawyer who was trying to learn the whereabouts of my father, but there was no news.

Then in 1944 and 1945, the Nazis started to lose their ground: the Allies were marching into Czechoslovakia from the west and the Russians from the East. It now became very important to my mother to seek help locating my father and getting him home. Dr. Kral (her German lawyer) recommended a JUdr. Porshe in Munich Germany who initiated a process in which she would give up her rights to all of their properties to the Nazi government in exchange for father's release. The hardest part was locating Father.

While my mother was experiencing the most harrowing time of her life, I was attending a private business school in the capitol city Brno, Moravia from 1944-45. This school was located across from the main railroad station of Brno on a second floor. Later, as the city was being bombed, my second year of schooling was held in an abandoned cafe. The bar was removed and desks were moved in. Because of the Nazi occupation, knowing the German language was essential. In our daily class routine, we had a mandatory lesson in German, be it German shorthand, German business correspondence, German bookkeeping, German conversation, and one day, reading the German newspaper. Because we were being readied for the business world, we attended school in business attire. This meant a business suit, hat, and gloves.

The first year at business school, I stayed at a convent with other female students. During the winter months, the Mother Superior decided that as young ladies we should learn how to dance. Her choice was to have the ballet choreographer from the opera house to teach us social dancing. At the graduation dancing lessons, I remember that I put together an evening of skits! It was fun dancing with the master ballet choreographer from the Brno Opera House At one point, he asked me to dance a waltz with him and we danced!. WOW! It sure was a thrill especially since I was always interested in ballet.

My second year of business school, Mother found housing for me in a dormitory-like facility outside of the city of Brno. The name of the facility was Americka Domovina (American Homestead). To this day, I have no idea how she found this place. But now, it is too late to ask. These two buildings were the gift of an American philanthropist, Mr, Severin, to enable young people studying different crafts to have a safe place to live. There were two large buildings, I believe 2-3 stories high and each equipped with a staff. One building housed young men the other, young women. Each had bedrooms with several beds and dressers. The main building, which was the young men's, had the main kitchen and a dining room. This is where we all gathered for the evening meal. Breakfasts were cooked and served in each building separately. Each building had a house-mother. We also had a study hall where we met to study which also served as the dining room for our breakfasts. This room also had a piano and several of us enjoyed playing it as we sang during evening hours. The home was surrounded by a cherry orchard which we helped to harvest. I remember one time when the war was getting close to the end, we were in the cherry trees and saw the Allied planes flying over our heads. Instead of seeking shelter, we all cheered them on!

Americka Domovina dormitory for students studying in Brno.

As students, we were required to attend rallies when Goering or other Nazi officers were in town. The speeches were held at a local opera house. While listening to the speeches, a Nazi officer would walk in the aisles to make sure that we all did the Nazi salute! We students were not safe on the streets either. If a Hitler-Jugen (Hitler's Youth) in his uniform felt a citizen was in his way, he could shoot that person on the spot. They wore beige uniforms with the Swastika, so they were easily recognizable.

While we were under Nazi occupation, the Czech people still voted for certain members of our government. I remember that, as students, if we wished to vote, we had to return to our hometowns to do so. As this was impossible, all we could do was sit and listen to the election results as they were broadcast on the radio.

The facility was surrounded by a pleasant wooded area with walking paths which we took advantage of quite often, especially on sunny days. On the main path, I remember, there was a little chapel erected to honor St. Anthony. It was not used for any religious services, but more for stopping and meditation. It was never open; the tall iron gates were always closed.

St. Anthony Chapel

Our day began with breakfast served in our dining room, after which we had to walk some distance to the main street to catch a street car. We used this public transportation to attend various schools in town. We also held several plays and cultural evenings in the boys' dormitory hall, which was always fun. I remember one time, there was to be a fun evening with skits I did not have any part in. I had sprained my ankle and would not be able to attend because the buildings were separated with a small distance and it would have been difficult for me to walk there. I was so touched by my roommates when they insisted on CARRYING me there, just so I can attend. Little did I know that part of a one act, I was the one being made fun off! They did not want to miss my reaction to this cruel joke! Oh well.

My roommates at Americka Domovina. I am the fourth in the line.

Since we returned home at different times each day, supper was served at 7:00 pm. One day on my way home from business school, I had a frightful experience. I missed my street car stop, so had to keep going to the next stop. I was sure I could return to the dormitory by walking through the brush. I got off at the next stop and started up the hill. It was quite steep, rocky, and dusty, and the tall grass and small bushes were scratching my legs, but I kept on climbing. All of a sudden I had the creepiest feeling. I looked around and noticed a middle aged man following me. At first it did not bother me, I was thinking perhaps he, too had missed his stop. I kept on walking, but the distance between me and him was getting shorter and shorter. I speeded up and so did he! By this time, the look on his face became strained and his breathing got louder, but he continued trying to catch up with me! Well, I was not going to wait to see his face close to mine. Somehow I got an extra strength to my step and length to my stride and was able to put him way back behind me as I scrambled toward safety! By this time, I was out of breath, but I was SAFE!!! Thank God! St. Anthony's chapel was a wonderful sight to see as I knew that the dormitory buildings would soon be in view.

Of course there were some wonderful memories of my life during those years. It was there that I met a young man who was to share a chapter of my life. He was wonderful, of course, charming, always smiling, and studying engineering in college. He was from Moravia, same state as me, had blond hair, blue eyes, played saxophone. We met the first time in my home town of Korycany while he was there with his band of musicians playing for a dance. Somehow though, even though we had met earlier, neither of us remembered it. It might be that our first meeting was in Brno in the Americka Domovina. Later, after we tried to remember, he confessed that he knew that Korycany was my home town, and therefore he loved to go there to play with his band. Obviously, this did not leave any impression on me at that time. This I have learned from the many letters I wrote to him after I began my new life in the United States which I will explain later. We spent much time together, having suppers, strolling on the grounds, and studying together, though he had more studying to do than me. On weekends, we went exploring the town of Brno, especially the churches and the architecture, attended operas, ballets and movies, just the wonderful things that young people do, wanting to spent every moment they can together. We in particular were fond of the Orion Constellation when watching the evening skies. We promised each other that no matter where we would be in the future, we would always look up and think of each other when we saw Orion. Such dreamers! He left the dormitory after one year when he graduated, and I stayed on for another year.

I attended the private business school for two years, graduating in 1944. After returning home, I was employed as a secretary at a local agricultural supply business from August 2, 1944 to Aug.1,1945.

During the retreat of the Nazis, the troops were on the move through villages. By this time Hitler had mobilized the Romanians. I remember the convoys of Russian troops going thru our town. They used wagons pulled by horses. Part of their armies were women, to keep the soldier boys happy. I could see the "girls" laying on top of the wagons in only their underwear! I heard about these "ladies" wearing silky nightgowns after they raided the big cities while attending opera presentations. They thought they were evening gowns! Many of the Romanian soldiers are buried in my town's cemetery. When these retreating armies were going through the towns and had to stay overnight, the officers were housed in private citizens' homes. The soldiers looked for a large home to accommodate them. I remember that we once had a Romanian SS officer staying at our home. We had to vacate one bedroom for him. During the night, his sergeant sat in front of the bedroom door to guard him. They also brought in food for Mother to cook. We all had to sit at the table to eat the meal with them. It was a guarantee that the food was not poisoned by the cook. My mother and I believe we ate horse meat that evening.

These pictures were taken from my Uncle Julius' apartment building attic window in Prague as the Germans were retreating..

By May of 1945, the war had ended and the Nazis were defeated. My father came home from the labor/ concentration camp. It was spring and new life was beginning for our family, our nation, and the whole world. We were able to breathe again, free of the Nazi oppression and the fear and hopelessness. Father rarely talked about his time away from home. It seemed that he did not want to remember.

There were times, here and there, when he would mention certain events. For example, one time he described the prisoners' cells. A cell was shared by several prisoners. The commode was in the corner with no privacy wall. Another time, he talked about the rationing of food. One chunk of bread to last the whole day was given with morning coffee. Then there was soup for lunch and maybe soup or something else for supper. Most of the prisoners ate the bread as soon as they received it, with nothing left for the rest of the day. It was no wonder that they scavenged scraps from the kitchen - the peelings from potatoes and other discarded food items – which they encountered on the way to their outdoor time! Hunger has no rationalizing. Father always believed in exercise and did so every time he had a chance to keep fit. He did some sort of calisthenics, moving his arms and legs. He still felt he was lucky because, being a shoemaker by trade, he was useful to the Nazi guards. After all, they all wore high boots and probably only had a one pair issued them, so they were in constant need of being repaired. My father was safe in a shoemaker shop on the premises of the camp and was doing what he knew how to do best. He was sheltered and probably reasonably warm. Even so, he lost weight and experienced weakness. I recall, when he came home, he weighed less than 100 lbs. and his arm muscles were the size of a walnut! Another time, while father was reminiscing, he told us that many of the prisoners and guards were infected with clothes lice. He had seen a Nazi officer scraping the lice of his boots with a knife! YUCK!

When father was released in Hamburg to go home, he was given 10 Marks (German currency). He told us how his release had come about. When the Russians were marching across Europe, the Nazis did not want them to see the camps, and so they were evacuating the prisoners by going west. The prisoners walked, of course, and this later became known as the Death March. Father told us about the conditions of the prisoners. Many suffered from dysentery, and when they had to relieve themselves, they stepped off the road. When they did so, the guards would shoot them. One less prisoner to care for and to feed! Thank God for my father's endurance and discipline. When they arrived in Hamburg, they were housed in the penitentiary. They arrived there on April 23. On April 25, Father heard his name was being paged, "Johann Tesař, Johann Tesař!" to which he answered, "Hir, Hir (here, here)"immediately, wondering what this was all that about? He got his answer, "You are being released to go home!"

I have a document issued by ITS Internationaler Suchdienst Postfach 1410 Grose Alee 5-9 34454 Bad Arolsen Deutchland, dated 10-4-2008. It states that my father's arrival at Hamburg-Fuhlsbuttel was on March 23, 1945 and that his release was on March 27. 1945.

By the way, I must explain about this letter. In 2000 I started researching about my father's imprisonment. I did not have much to go on, just some notes of my father. I read books on different labor camps and concentration camps, and I wrote letters to numerous organizations that were suggested to me.

One of my father's documents was *Comitee Internationale De La Croix-Rouge*(International Red Cross Committee). I do not know how he came to have this document, but it was received by RA Dr Porsche in Munchen (Munich), Germany on May 29. 1962. On the back of this document, Father listed a history of his arrest on January 12 by German Police at his home in Korycany, Czechoslovakia. It continues, that he was taken to the Brno (Brunn) city prison. After his trial he mentions the towns he was taken to by box car: SUMPERK, BRESLAU, POSEN, DANZIG STETIN, GOLNOW after that to HAMBURG, from where he was released.

I have written to all those towns inquiring of some records of my father but always got an "general printed postcard" back, with apologies, NO RECORDS OF Jan Tesař. All I wanted was some documentation of him being there. Much later I found out, that all these towns had labor camps. They were constructed and used as long as the need was there .Then the "workers" were sent to another labor camp. No wonder there were no records, but it hurt when I received answers to my inquiries with such cold and impersonal post cards.

According to German documents issued by *Bezirksant fur Wiedergutmechung*, Trier, Germany that I found in my father's papers:

Arrested January 12, 1942 in the town of Korycany at home by German Criminal Police

Imprisoned in Brunn (Brno)

taken to Kraukenhaus (hospital)

back to prison in Brunn (Brno)

1944 transferred to Breslau

then to Danzig- Stettin

over to Golnov and Hamburg, Germany

discharged from Hamburg in April 1945

| Anfragende Stelle: | F-30 a |

COMITÉ INTERNATIONALE DE LA CROIX-ROUGE
Service International de Recherches - International Tracing Service - Internationaler Suchdienst
Arolsen/Waldeck - Deutschland

( ) Inhaftierungsbescheinigung ( ) Krankenpapiere
( ) Aufenthaltsbescheinigung ( ) Auskunft über Auswanderung
( ) Suchantrag ( ) Sterbeurkunde

Fragen: Antworten:

I. **Personalangaben:** im Konzentrationslager   im D. P.-Lager
(Tarnnamen)

1. Namen/Mädchenname _____ kein -

2. Vornamen _____

3. bei Namensänderung nach dem Krieg
jetziger Name u. Vorname _____

4. Geburtsdaten (Tag, Monat, Jahr) _____

5. Geburtsort _____

6. Beruf _____

7. Religion _____

8. Staatsangehörigkeit _____

9. letzte Anschrift vor der Inhaftierung
(auch Straße und Hausnummer) _____

10. Namen der Eltern (auch Mädchenname
der Mutter) _____

11. Familienstand z. Z. der Inhaftierung _____

    a) Familienstand heute? _____

    b) Falls verheiratet, Vor- und Mädchennamen
    der Ehefrau / Vorname des
    Ehemannes? evtl. 1. Ehe - 2. Ehe _____

    c) Ort und Datum der Eheschließung? _____

12. Unterschriftsprobe   wie im Konzentrationslager   wie im D. P.-Lager

bitte wenden!

II. Angaben über Inhaftierung:

13. Verhaftet am: 12. Januar Korytany durch: Deutsch polizie
Eingeliefert in das: Brün Häftl. Nr. 2 Block Nr. 2
am: einweisende Stelle: in Erinnerung
Überstellt zum: Sunport weiter Häftl. Nr. Breslau Block Nr.
Überstellt zum: Posen am: Danzig Häftl. Nr. Stetin Block Nr.
Überstellt zum: Golnow am: bis Häftl. Nr. nach Block Nr.
Befreit, entlassen oder gestorben am: Hamburg + entlassen.

III. Angaben über Aufenthalt nach dem Kriege:

14. Sämtliche Aufenthaltsorte und -daten nach dem Kriege: in Korytany — und in Spital — Ungarisch Hradisch, und Brno — und
15. Nummer des CM/1-Bogens und die DP-Reg. Nr.?
16. Auswanderung erfolgte:
   a) wann: zur hause — Korytany. Mähren.
   c) wohin:
   d) wie (Schiffsnamen - Flugnummer):
   e) mit welchen Familienangehörigen:
   f) unter welchem Namen? Jan Tesař 2643 S. Lawndale ave
17. Jetzige Anschrift? Chicago, Ill. U.S.A.

IV. Bei Anforderungen von Krankenpapieren:

18. Für die Zeit der Inhaftierung KL (Krankenbau) Ort: verloren bei umziehen
19. Für die Zeit nach dem Kriege DP (Hospital):

V. Sonstiges

20. Anschrift und Aktenzeichen der zuständigen Wiedergutmachungsbehörde (Bei Anforderung von ITS Inhaftierungs- und Aufenthaltsbescheinigungen unbedingt anzugeben.)

[stamp: 29. Mai 1962 RA Dr. Porsche München 5]

Jan Tesař
(Unterschrift)

Jan Tesař repatriation papers. On the back of this document it states, that he has given up his right to repatriation and to add the amount due to him to the Fund. He felt, this should be given to the families, who were not as lucky as he was, him returning home, while prisoners did not.

Below are some things found on the internet concerning some of these locations:

Breslau

http://www.edwardvictor.com/ *Breslau (Wroclaw, Poland) was a subcamp of Gross Rosen which supplied labor to various companies operating plants in the area.*

http://en.wikipedia.org/wiki/History_of_Wroclaw/

In addition, a network of concentration camps and forced labour camps, or Arbeitslager, was established in the district around Breslau, to serve the city's growing industrial concerns, including FAMO, Junkers and Krupp. The total number of prisoners held at such camps exceeded many tens of thousands.[51] *Official Nazi estimates reported 43,950 forced labourers in 1943 and 51,548 in 1944, most of them being Poles.*[52]

http://www.rogermoorhouse.com/*Conditions within Breslau's ZAL are difficult to determine; but patchy evidence allows the drawing of some tentative conclusions. Czech workers in the Krupp plant in Markstädt received some sort of payment and originally could leave the camp with permission but had their leave allowance cut following repeated escape attempts. Naturally conditions varied from camp to camp, from month to month, from inmate to inmate, and suffered a general deterioration as the war progressed. However, given that Polish and Czech workers evidently received payment and leave, it would seem reasonable to conclude that conditions in at least some of Breslau's Zwangsarbeitslager were not universally bad....As has been shown, figures from the Krupp plant at Markstädt reveal a workforce in which Czechs, Italians and Frenchmen formed the majority for a considerable time.*

Danzig

http://en.wikipedia.org/wiki/List_of_prisoner-of-war_camps_in_Germany#XVII_Army_Corps_.28Danzig.29*The "camp" consists of barges moored on the bank of the Vistula River, each containing from 100 to 500 men. The administration block, kitchen, and other facilities of the camp are on shore. Men from the failed Irish Brigade were sent here.*

Stettin (Szczecin, Poland)

Szczecin is a port city and transportation hub. Possibly this was a location to change trains?

Golnow

http://pl.wikipedia.org/wiki/Goleni%C3%B3w

Goleniów (just after the war Gołonóg [1], German Gollnow) - a city in the western part of the province. West Pomeranian in Goleniów district, situated on the river Ina, at Coastland Szczecin, 35 km north-east of Szczecin

Hamburg-Fuhlsbüttel, Germany

http://en.tracesofwar.com/article/4891/Fuhlsb%FCttel-Concentration-Camp.html *The old prison complex of Fuhlsbüttel, was used by the Gestapo until April 1945. During the winter 1944/1945, Fuhlsbüttel served as sub camp for the Neuengamme concentration camp. Almost 500 persons perished here in the period 1933-1945.*

And here is some conflicting information from

http://www.memorialmuseums.org/

From 1936 on, the Fuhlsbüttel concentration camp was renamed »police prison«, however, the conditions for the prisoners didn't change. It continued to be administered by the Gestapo and remained in existence until 1945. On October 25, 1944, the SS additionally set up a satellite camp of the Neuengamme concentration camp in a part of the Fuhlsbüttel prison building. About 1,500 prisoners were kept there, and conducted forced labour in construction and clean-up work on buildings damaged by air raids. The strenuous work and insufficient supplies resulted in the death of 2 to 3 prisoner deaths per day. In all, over 270 prisoners perished, thus making Fuhlsbüttel one of the satellite camps with the highest death rate in Northern Germany.

Fuhlsbüttel concentration camp   Gatehouse

On February 15, 1945, the SS dissolved the camp and brought the prisoners to the Dessauer Ufer satellite camp.

http://openbuildings.com/buildings/dessauer-ufer-profile-27096

Dessauer Ufer *was a Nazi Germany subcamp of the Neuengamme concentration camp. The camp opened in mid-July 1944 for 1,000 Czechs and Hungarian Jewish woman selected from Auschwitz-Birkenau. After a month 500 more Polish-Jewish women were forced to work in the Geilenberg programme as oilman to rescue the refineries from Rhenania Ossag (Shell), Ebano-Oehler (Esso), J. Schindler, Jung-Öl, and Blohm + Voss. On 13 September 1944 the women were transported to the camps Hamburg-Sasel, Wedel and Hamburg-Neugraben. 2000 prisoners of war were brought to the camp. The clearing up work for the refineries continued, some inmates were digging anti-tank obstacles at Hittfeld. A 25 October 1944 air raid partly destroyed the camp. 150 inmates died and the SS transported the men to the subcamp Fuhlsbüttel. On 15 February 1945, 800 prisoners were transported back from Fuhlsbüttel to the camp to produce petrol for Jung-Öl. On October 25, 1945 the SS closed the camp transporting the inmates to the camp Stalag X-B at Sandbostel.*

Dessauer Ufer

ITS
International Tracing Service
Service International de Recherches
Internationaler Suchdienst

ITS Internationaler Suchdienst · Postfach 1410 · 34444 Bad Arolsen

Große Allee 5-9 · 34454 Bad Arolsen · Deutschland
Tel. +49 5691 629-0 · Fax +49 5691 629-501
email@its-arolsen.org · www.its-arolsen.org

Mrs Zee Kiszkan
7567 Schow Road
HOLTON, MI 49425-9527
USA

Bad Arolsen, 9th April 2008
SCH/eued

Our Reference
(please quote)
T/D – 2 222 498

Your letter to the German Embassy,
Washington, received here on
21st August 2000 and your letter
of 14th September 2001

**Your inquiry concerning
your father, Mr Jan/Johan TESAR, born on 13.9.1883 in Malinky**

Dear Mrs Kiszkan,

We are referring to your above-mentioned inquiries and advise you that we have checked the documentary material kept here, based on the information that you were kind enough to provide.

The following details could be taken from the documents of the International Tracing Service:

TESAR, Johan, born on 13.9.1883 in Koritschan,
nationality: Czechoslovakian,

was confined to the penitentiary Hamburg-Fuhlsbüttel
on 23rd March 1945 and released to Koritschan on
27th March 1945.

The files mention: "Crime: Breach of war work regulation."

Unfortunately, we do not hold any further information.

There exist institutions in the USA, which may be of help in the search for information about your father. We think in particular of the United States Holocaust Memorial Museum in Washington, D.C. and the American Red Cross, Holocaust and War Victims Center in Baltimore, M.D.

We remain

with kind regards,

Martina Saueracker
For the Archives

WOW! Finally, father was free. Of course, walking was the only way for him to return home since the railroads were destroyed, no trains were running, and the roads were bombed. He hitchhiked, sometimes cars, sometimes farm wagons, mostly he walked and by generosity of people, mainly farmers, who offered him food and lodging in barns, he made it home in less than a week.

Oh how I remember that day of his return!

We knew that the Nazi occupation was coming to an end, and Mother had the lawyers working on locating my father with hopes to have him home again. We did not know when and how this would happen, but we were hoping that he would come home on the train! I had a friend that worked on our local train which connected with the main train. So I gave this young friend instruction: IF and WHEN he spotted my father to run as fast as he could to come and tell us! Of course, we had hopes that it would happen soon, but days went by with no news and it seemed so hopeless. Then, the day before Easter, everyone was at home busily cleaning and getting ready for Easter when my friend appeared at the door with the glorious announcement, "Your father is on the train!!!!!"

We dropped everything and hurried to meet him! Oh how wonderful to see my father again! He was so thin and his clothes were dirty and in shreds, but he still had his big smile! Mother took him in the back yard to have him take off all the clothes to burn them. His bath was ready for him and after, we were again a family together! I remember that even though father was now home and food was plentiful, he was aware that he must control his intake. Here goes again my father's discipline. He controlled how much food to eat as he knew that his stomach had gotten smaller, and he must not overeat. On a sad note, Grandmother had passed away while he was gone and was missing from Father's homecoming celebrations.

While still at home, during the early year of 1945 the principle of the high school who had taken an interest in me earlier because of my drawing, enrolled me in the entrance tests at Commercial Art School in Brno, the capitol city of Moravia. He persuaded my parents to let me go because, he said, I needed to pursue my interest in art.

I was excited! It was a daylong process with tests in different mediums, some of which I had never heard. There were 400 applicants, and I did not think I had a chance. At the end of the day, I was exhausted, but I still had to take the two-hour train ride home. Several weeks later, the school principle came to our home to joyfully announce that I had been selected to attend the school!

Because the art school was quite a distance from my home, it was not practical to commute daily, and I was housed at a boarding school dormitory. It was exciting to see and learn all the different areas of art. I especially enjoyed designing printed fabric and then using that fabric to design an article of clothing best suited for it. We visited factories where different bolts of materials were made, and that was interesting as well. We did outdoor sketching and figure drawings. One time we sketched a muscular man from the visiting circus. We also studied different types of lettering but that did not appeal to me. I even applied for job related to painting on material, but while I was waiting for the interview, I saw the repetitive designs that they were working on. That was not for me, so I left before the interviewer came out! I stayed at the commercial art school for one year, after which my parents decided that this would not get me a job and took me out. Even the pleas from the director of the school could not persuade my parents. Oh well, such is life.

So the year 1946 found me working as a typist of insurance policies for Fireman Insurance Company in Brno. I only stayed there for six months due to sexual harassment by my boss. I started in the typist pool, typing out insurance policies. From time to time, the bosses of different department would come in and pick some girls to work in their departments. I guess I was lucky, because, one day, I was picked to work in a small claim office. My job consisted of locating the policies in the file room, when there was a claim. I also did some correspondence with the clients. There were only two other employees in the office plus the boss who, at times, wanted some typing done "after" working hours. HUH? I was DONE!

My sister Miroslava and I in 1946. I am 20 and she is 17.

Then, in December 1946, I was hired at a wholesale aircraft fuel company where my friend, Jarka, was employed.. We decided to find us an apartment together. So we packed up, hopped on the train, and headed to Brno (the capitol city of Moravia). We arrived in the late afternoon but had no idea where to find an apartment. A very kind lady in the luggage storage department at the railroad depot gave us the address of a friend of hers, with the hope that we might get a place there. So we embarked on the search of the address and finally found it. The lady was very friendly, but she only had one small room with one bed.

We decided to stay the night and start the apartment hunt again in the morning. The bed was a single with one blanket, but the blanket was very scratchy. We had no choice but to try to get some sleep. The itching and scratching eventually became unbearable, and, when we turned on the lights, there were bed bugs crawling on the walls and on the blanket! Hundreds of them! We went out onto the balcony hoping to sit out the night. The neighboring tenant heard us and came out to offer us her place. One of us could sleep with her in her bed and the other could sit at the table with her head on the table. We switched positions once during the night, and finally morning came!

Since we had left our luggage at the railroad station, we had to go there first. Another lady there gave us second lead on an apartment. We collected our luggage, got on the bus and headed out with high hopes. Since the war, many of the buildings were not livable due to the bombings. When we finally found the address, a plump, jovial lady answered the door. This place turned out to be quite nice. It was an apartment building with a courtyard. The second story was not damaged and had a large apartment which could have been at one time two apartments separated by a door. It had an entry hall where there was an electric two burner stove, a little sink with running water, a bathroom (no shower or bathtub) but a flushing toilet! A door opened to a very large room with two large windows facing the street below. It also had two beds, one against each of the side walls: paradise! And, hopefully NO BEDBUGS!!! The rent must have been reasonable for we moved in! We lived there almost two enjoyable years.

We attended the opera house at least once a week. Our tickets were for standing not seats. Sometimes, if there were seats to be had after the performance had started, we could sneak in with just a tip to the usher. We enjoyed many of the operas and ballets. I had quite a crush on the leading ballet performer. His name was Viktor Malcev, and he came from the Bolshoi Ballet in Moscow. One of my roommates at the Severin Dormitory knew him personally which helped me get behind stage after the performance to meet him. I got to know him and, needless to say, I was in seventh heaven! I invited him to our apartment for a little get-together and he came! We served watermelon and snacks, and we shared a bottle of wine. It was the first and only time I got to talk to him, but I saw him perform many times at the opera house. My roommate, Jarka, of course, was elated to get to know him as well. I recently was able to find on the internet that Victor was the chief choreographer at the North Bohemia Theater in Usti nad Labem in Czechoslovakia from 1945-1947, but nothing after that. I wonder if I can find him on Facebook?

Because the Russians were starting to take over, my father started to think about returning to USA. He brought his naturalization papers to the USA Consulate in Prague, Czechoslovakia. There he received some crushing news: he had missed the date of re-registering and had lost his USA citizenship! He was devastated! He explained to the Consular that we, his two daughters, wanted to go back and how could he let us go by ourselves? The only solution they gave him was to apply for a Czechoslovak passport. My sister and I had to go to the USA Consulate in Prague to be re-instated as USA citizens. Since we were not able to return to USA due to the war, the law allowed us to continue our citizenship. The phrasing was, "Due to the War therefore inability to return." By this time I had completely forgotten the English language. So I was sent to city of Brno to attend a foreign language school. I only had two or three months to learn English before my planned trip back to USA in January 1948. The class was taught by a British teacher with a strong English accent and did not really prepare me for American English.! By now, my friend, Olda, and I met again and were making plans for our future which was so very unstable at this time because of my departure in January. We promised each other faithfulness with hopes to be together again. How foolish of us.

1947 Our last Christmas in Czechoslovakia

My sister's and my reinstatement of our USA citizenships at the American Consulate in Prague was quite a moving experience. The American Consul, I'm sorry that I did not write down his name, was the one who performed the ceremony. My sister and I were instructed to put our hands over our hearts and listen, since we did not speak English anymore, to the Consular as he recited the Pledge of Allegiance next to the American flag. As I recall, this was a quite solemn and moving experience.

1949 passport photo

PART SIX:

Back in the USA

PASSENGER MANIFEST

CARRIER: PAN AMERICAN AIRWAYS INC.
ORIGINATED AT: BRUSSELS BELGIUM
DESTINED TO: WASHINGTON U.S.A.
DATE: January 18th 1948
PLANE NO: NC/88837
FLIGHT NO: 113/17
PASSENGERS EMBARKING AT: BRUSSELS BELGIUM
PASSENGERS DESTINED TO: NEW YORK U.S.A.

#	NAME	TICKET NO.	AGE	SEX	NATIONALITY / PASSPORT NO.	OCCUPATION	PERS. WT.	NO. BAGS	BAG WT.
1	TEBAR, Zdenka — 2624 West 50th Str., Chicago Ill.	269PA28647	21	F	U.S.A. 944 1/2/48	U.S. CIT.	71	2	30
2	FROSVIO, Jan — 80 Broadway New York 5 N.Y.	263PA29646	40	M	CZECH V-229912 2963/7772/46	I-466 HEAD TAX EXEMPT C			
3	SZABADOS, Yolande — 811 Lane Str, Detroit Michigan	263PA41315	19	F	U.S.A. 968/1/12/48	U.S. CIT.	74	5	85 A
4	SZABADOS, Mary — same address	263PA41315	14	F	U.S.A. 969/1/12/48	U.S. CIT.	65		HEAD TAX DUE
5	SZABADOS, Margaret — same address	263PA41315	48	F	CZECH 1647 I-183445 I-466 NDIV				
6	STEINER, Miklow — Transit to Australia, Sidney, Edge Cliff, New South Head Rd.	265PA28679	28	M	HUNGARIAN V-20821 38961/538160	I-466 TO 330 HEAD TAX EXEMPT			
7	SYCHRAVA, Lev — 606-1775 Broadway New York N.Y.	261PA19925	58	M	CZECH 568/47 T-1092 I-466 N-712	HEAD TAX EXEMPT	85		

All s/m PAX from flite 181/17 Ex. PRAGUE.

Lines 2.3.4.5.6.
Balance — Transitory

U.S. Immigrant Inspector
JAN 19 1948

TOTALS: NO. PAX 7 — 532 — 10 — 170

PREPARED BY: L.B.SAB.

NOTE: PASSENGER DEBARKATIONS EN ROUTE—INDICATE(D) BY RED "OFF AT (PLACE)" STAMP

I left for the United States on January 18th, 1948, from Ruzyna Airport in Prague, Czechoslovakia on Pan American Airlines. Mother, my uncle Julius, and I arrived at the airport early in the morning because the plane was supposed to depart at 10 am. There must have been some problem because we didn't leave until afternoon.

Instead of arriving in New York City, we only made it as far as Brussels, Belgium where we were housed in a hotel to continue our flight the next afternoon. Since we had some free time in the morning, one of the passengers suggested we explore the town which we did by hiring a taxi. It was a good time!

Our next flight took us as far as London where we were given lunch and continued to Shannon, Ireland. After refueling, I think, we were finally on our way. Later I found out, that we did not take the regular route because of inclement weather.

Our plane traveled south and arrived at the Islands of Azores. It was night, and so I did not see much of the island. The most I remember about this stop was how warm it was there. After all, I had left Czechoslovakia in January! We were able to roam the airport, and then we boarded the plane again.

By now it was getting light outside, and I recall flying over the island of Bermuda! Oh what a sight! It almost looked unreal! A beautiful, green island, dotted with stark white buildings, and surrounded by a beautiful blue ocean. It looked like a postcard!

When we finally touched down in New York at LaGuardia Airport, I was glad to be on solid ground again, for I did not have a pleasant time on the airplane. I had found out, what those little paper bags were for in the pocket of the seat in front of me! It was evening, so all that I saw of New York were the lights of buildings and streets below. I remember wanting to purchase something at the airport, but I only had paper money. A very pleasant lady at a counter gave me change, a LOT of change!! I wonder what the denomination was that I had given her! Also I had to give up an apple that my father had wanted me to give to my new family. He grew that apple and was so proud of it! Of course it had to be taken away from me, because of the no produce rule.

Oh well. I continued my trip by plane to Chicago Midway Airport where I was met by my parents' friends, Hynek and Emily Selucky. I would be making my home with their family until the time when my parents would arrive.

You may remember Hynek Selucky, the shoemaker who my parents helped to move from Texas to Chicago. So now, he was able to return my parents' kindness when I needed a place to stay when I returned to USA in 1948! He was married now to Emily with four children (he also made a trip to the "Old Country" to get a wife in about 1935). I remember him visiting our family in Korycany at that time.

The Seluckys took me in as one of their own. My "aunt" Emily was more like an older sister to me, she was not much older than me, and their children had fun teaching me the American language! My aunt taught me how to make the bed, which was much different than I had been taught. The children all played musical instruments. Laddie, the oldest, played violin, Uncle played an accordion, and I played the piano. We had several "musical" evenings. Emily, Marta and the youngest, Frankie, played also.

My cousins, Jarka (Jerry) and her sister Martha Navratil, visited often and many Sundays took me out for the afternoon to explore Jackson Park by Lake Michigan. I also was invited to their home every Tuesday for supper! I loved fresh pineapple, as I had never had it before, so my aunt tried to always have some for me! After supper, my cousins and I would take a walk in the neighborhood (55th and California). We enjoyed looking in the picture windows of the American houses. In Czechoslovakia, most families did not have a living room, and certainly not a huge window through which all could see the homes' interiors. It was the custom for families to congregate in the kitchens. Now, looking back, I am embarrassed at our "peeping Tom" behavior. Other times, in the evening, we would walk to an electronics store and stand with the crowd watching the television through the store window. When mother learned of these visits, she was so pleased because these were the only "blood" relations that she had in the US, and it was important to her to have this relationship.

My second cousins in 1950. From the left: Jarina Navratil, Aunt Betty Navratil, Martha Navratil-Schmidt, Aunt Betty (Elizabeth) was mother's first cousin.

Within a week of my arrival, I was hired at Skala National Bank in Chicago. My "uncle" Hynek found an ad in the Czech newspaper Hlasatel the day after I arrived. The bank was looking for a Czech speaking person to work in their travel department. Who else was more qualified than me? After all, I had been educated for office work and spoke Czech! Never mind that my English was something else to be desired. Since it was a Czech bank in a Czech neighborhood, all of the employees (15 of them) spoke Czech. Well, enough so that I felt I at home there. Honestly, when I look back to this time, I wonder, where in the world did I get this gumption? My salary was $ 25.00 a week, and with the taxes and SS taken out, I received $23.75. I spent 18c daily for my round-trip bus fare, and I gave my host family $6 per week for room and board. My aunt, Emily, packed me lunch of a sandwich and a little bottle of milk. $10 each week went into my savings account (always the habit). The rest I could spend anyway that I wanted!

My job was arranging passage and general travel, mainly to Czechoslovakia for our clients. Many of them lived out of town and even out of state. I took dictations in shorthand from my boss, Mr. Kuzel, in Czech to correspond with our clientele. I prepared official papers for immigrants to secure visas to the USA. We also sent money to relatives for our customers. I was able to go to downtown Chicago by bus to various airline and steamship companies to get reservations and also to several consulates to apply for visas for our customers.. I even personally wrote by hand airline flight tickets!

Since my father lost his American citizenship, he had to travel on Czech passport and also my mother. Also, they needed an affidavit from an American citizen (me) to enter the USA. My sister had been reinstated as an American citizen, like me, and was coming with them. It took some time, until November, 1948, for them to arrange passage with the Cunard White Star Steamship Company.

I received many letters, mainly from Father, keeping me informed of the progress of moving. There were many trips to the USA Consulate in Prague and to the Cunard White Star Steamship Line to arrange the trip. It took several trips to different offices to arrange the emigration. Father wrote to me about the packing, the decisions about what to bring with them, and what was important to establish a new household. Their custom-made furniture, the piano, the original paintings (which Mother so loved), and the imported carpets had to be sold or left behind. Uncle Julius ended up with some of these in his Prague apartment. I only now realize what a sacrifice our parents made, just so we girls could return to our homeland. Finally, there were four huge steamship trunks packed. These trunks were the same ones they used when they moved from Chicago to Czechoslovakia in 1931. I still have two of them!

Since things were being taken out of the country, an officer had to come to the house and evaluate the content. Export dues were imposed and had to be paid before the trunks were sealed and shipped to Cunard White Star. Imagine that! Paying export dues on one's own possessions! But this was the beginning of the Communist regime. The whole process must have been heart-breaking. They were not able to sell the house because it was too large, so they were looking for renters, at least for the beginning, until Uncle Julius would be able to dispose of it. Even the rent was regulated by the government and could not exceed their set rules. There were many arrests and penalties for not following the "suggested" amount for rental.. All of this, I learned from the letters I received from my parents which I still have.

This is a label from one of the trunks.

Before my family arrived, I was fortunate to be able to buy a small house for them. As always, God in His infinite wisdom! There is an interesting story about that house. Soon after I arrived in Chicago, my "uncle" Hynek, took me to visit a distant relative of mine. This man, Zizlavsky, was some sort of an uncle to my father. When our family lived in Chicago in the late twenties, we visited him quite often though I do not personally remember. By now, he was a widower and his two daughters were married and living on the East Coast somewhere in New York. We had a pleasant visit. Imagine my surprise when shortly after that visit, we received news that this uncle had died!

2432 S. HOMAN
CHICAGO, ILL

My uncle Hynek had a bright idea! Why not buy that little house and have it for my family? After all, they knew the house and location; it was in a Czech neighborhood which was important. So, after the funeral, he made arrangement to meet with the daughters and they were willing to sell! They even left some furniture behind and, lucky for me, the bank where I worked was willing to give me a mortgage! The house cost $6,800 Father had left about $2,000 in Chicago at the Lawndale Bank, so I had a down payment. So now, I was a home owner!

All I had to buy was a bed with mattress and boxed spring which Uncle Hynek helped me to purchase from a furniture store! The daughters also left a couch, a big round oak dining room table, and some chairs. There was also a gas stove (we had always used a wood stove in the old country), one of those highboys which were popular at the time. I purchased some drapes for the living room, paper ones from the Dime store which Mother immediately tore off the windows after their arrival in Chicago! Well, the drapes were priced reasonably and looked nice, or so I had thought!
Highboy stove

Mother's letters were always full of odd advice: how to behave and to be careful. After I purchased the house on Homan Avenue in Chicago, I wanted to stay there sometimes. Mother thought that was a good idea, not leaving the house empty, but was baffled why Mrs. Risky, my friend Frances' mother, did not approve of me staying there full-time. (I had met my dear friend, Frances, at the bank when the staff paired us two single young women together) My mother worried that I had done something wrong, maybe hurt the Selucky's feelings? She scolded me to be more appreciative which was really unfounded. Of course, I spent more time at the Risky house now and "my" house and did not have much time left to visit the Selucky's, my first home. Mother could not understand that I was now being more independent.

I spent lots of time and weekends with the Risky family. Once when Mrs. Risky had to have gallbladder surgery, I became the main cook for the family! I was the oldest. I stayed at their house often and shared a bedroom with Frances when we were not at "my" house.

Letters from Olda were coming pretty regularly, and he always had hopes of joining me in the USA. There would be 2-3 letters weekly full of hope and yearning. By now the Russians were in charge of the Czech lands. Like all of the young men, Olda was required to enroll in military for two years. The new Russian government was very reluctant to lose young people, so even after the required time in military, the prospects of Olda joining me in the US were becoming very dim. Before my parents left Czechoslovakia, Olda traveled to my hometown to visit my parents and officially ask for my hand .This was getting serious! On his second visit he brought an engagement ring to them to give me. So now, plans were getting more and more positive. If only the government would cooperate! The letters became our only hope and joy.

I enjoyed working at the bank, especially in my department for I only had one boss that gave me direct orders. Later on, I was on my own because my boss was transferred to another department. One of the perks in my department was that if our travel office could put together a group of ten travelers, I could get one FREE flight ticket to be the group leader! Soooo, that was my chance! My opportunity for a trip to Czechoslovakia would come in May 1949. Olda had to either pursue a passport or plan for us to get married at that time! He would take care of the wedding, and his mother started to plan a wedding reception. My uncle Julius would represent my mother and father and also act as a witness. Oh such a happy time of planning!

My family eventually booked passage on a ship named the S S Mauretania which was leaving from Cherbourg Harbor, France on Nov. 6. 1948. They had to travel by train from Czechoslovakia to Cherbourg through Paris, and I was to meet them at the main railroad station in Chicago 5 or 6 days later.

I was distressed when I went to the train station to pick them up and they weren't there. The immigration office employees at Union Station were very helpful. They discovered that there had been a dock workers' strike in New York, and, therefore, the ship had to travel to Halifax, Canada for them to disembark! It was a wonderful reunion once we finally were together several days later. According to some documents that I have in my procession, they all had to get inoculated against small pox. Also, from the same documents I found out that all of the booking was in my sister's name because she was the only American citizen in their group. It could be, also, that she was the only one who saved any of these documents. Interestingly, I found that they were assigned a cabin and also a place with a number for seating at meal times!

Border Crossings: From Canada to U.S., 1895-1956 about

Name:	**Jan Tesař**
Arrival Date:	11 Nov 1948
Port of Arrival:	Halifax, Nova Scotia, Canada
Ship Name:	Mauretania
Port of Departure:	Cherbourg, France
Age:	65
Birth Date:	abt 1883
Gender:	Male
Race/Nationality:	Slovak (Slovakian)

Reunited with Mom and Dad.

I was also happy to be reunited with my family. Father was able to find a shoemaker shop in the Czech neighborhood, where our little cottage was. By this time, he was 65 years old, and should have been retiring, but he was looking for a job to earn living!

This brings me, to another story. There was only ONE shoemaker repair shop available in this neighborhood and it was for sale. When the operator and father agreed on a price, Uncle Hynek loaned Father $ 1.500.00 to purchase the machinery. The building where the shop was located was a rental property and next to it was a liquor store. The same landlady owned the whole building. Father asked how was he going to pay the rent and the shop operator assured him not to worry because she came and collected the rent every month.

> **NEW MAN--**
> **but all-around EXPERIENCE**
> # Shoemaker
> 2554 S. Lawndale Ave., near 26th Street
>
> EXPERT SHOE REPAIR — ONE DAY SERVICE
>
> Residence:
> 2432 S. Homan Ave.
>
> **John Tesař**
>
> appreciates your patronage

A new shop and a new advertising blotter.

When 1st of the month came, an older lady walked into my father's shop. Thinking that she was a customer, my father politely asked if he could help her. Something looked very familiar about this lady's face and he gingerly said, "Anna?" To which she slowly replied, "Johann?" Lo and behold, they had been school mates in the one-room school in their Czech homeland in the little town of Malinky many, many years ago! Needless to say, their friendship was renewed and I remember her vividly. Later when I had children she loved to have them come over and served those fruit compote and juice in special delicate china Havilland cups! She was a widow by this time and childless, and she loved the little ones.

She and her husband had befriended a young man. I do not remember if he was an orphan, but they put him through medical school. He turned out to be a very successful doctor and never forgot their generosity and kindness to him, which he and his family amply returned.

Anna became indirectly our benefactor as well. When at one time, father mentioned to her that he would like to purchase a small property outside of Chicago to enjoy some fresh air and sunshine on weekends, she had an answer. Well, she had 40 acres of land in Holton, Michigan, and he was welcome to it! When father objected that it would be too far to travel for not having a car, with her permission, could he give it to his daughters who owned cars? To which she replied, "I don't care what you do with it, but that sounds reasonable!" So that is how we became the proud owners of 20 acres of the Holton land and eventually built a home and retired there! The other 20 acres Father gave to my sister, Miroslava, and her husband, Bohumil Kratky.

Eventually the month of May, 1949 came and my trip to Czechoslovakia leading a group of eager travelers was finally here. They were all looking to visiting with their families, and I was looking toward a new future! I had two weeks of vacation which was to change my life forever!

This is the group I traveled with.

> PAN AMERICAN WORLD AIRWAYS PHOTO
>
> TO VISIT THEIR HOMELAND
>
> Ten midwest Czech-Americans prepare to board a Pan American World Airways Clipper in New York en route to Prague, Czechoslovakia. Most of the group were born in Czechoslovakia and for practically all of them it was their first return since the war. The tour was led by Miss Zdenka Tesar (front row left) representing the Skala National Bank, 1817 S. Loomis St., Chicago.
>
> Thr group consisted of (left to right), front row — Miss Tesar, 2432 S. Homan St., Helen Smid, 2626 S. Keeler St., both of Chicago; Mary Janko, Medford, Wis.; Jan Mikulex, 1313 N. Julian St., Chicago and Joseph Hradex, Clarkson, Neb.; rear row — Emily Selucky, 2624 W. 59 St., Anna Ursin, 5125 W. Gunnison St., Bessie Melicharek, 5820 S. Richmond St., Olga Slaninka, 5134 S. Kenneth St., John Podolsky, 2057 W. James St., and James Lhotak, 2626 S. Keller St., all of Chicago.
>
> FROM PAN AMERICAN WORLD AIRWAYS
> LA GUARDIA FIELD, N. Y.
>
> A30590RW052549
> AX

Olda and Uncle Julius were waiting for me at the Prague airport. What a joyous meeting! The very next day, Olda and I went to the American Consulate for advice and directions for our wedding. There, we received disheartening news: If I married a Czech citizen I would automatically lose my USA citizenship and become a Czech citizen, even if the marriage was performed at the USA Consulate. This is not what either of us wanted to hear. The church would not marry us without the USA Consulate documentation. Sad, sad news, such a sinking deep hole in our hearts and such feelings of frustration and desperation! At least I did not bring a wedding dress. Mother thought a nice light grey 2 piece suit with a little veil would be more appropriate since I was traveling. She insisted on a veil for I deserved it.

> Zdeňka L. Tesařová
> Oldřich Mrázek
>
> dovolují si oznámiti své zasnoubení
>
> CHICAGO   KVĚTEN 1949   LOMNICE U TIŠNOVA

Engagement announcement

Several days later, the three of us took a train to Olda's home and his hometown of Lomnice u Tisnova in Morava. There we were welcomed by his whole family whom I had never met before. The preparations for our wedding reception were at full speed, but the news we brought was not what they had expected. In spite of the change in developments, the party-planning continued. Now, instead of a wedding, we were having an elaborate engagement party with all the relatives. Afterwards I stayed on, and Julius returned to Prague. My returning flight was at the end of the following week from Prague, so I spent a delightful several days with the family, bike riding, visiting local interesting historical places and just getting to know them. But all good things must end.

We returned to Prague a couple of days before my departure and did some site seeing. One of our stops was St. Vitus Cathedral. If we could not get legally married, we would say the marriage vows to each other in that holy place. And that we did. Disregarding the visiting crowds of school children and visitors, we sat in a pew closest to the altar. We held hands and, I have to admit, some tears were streaming down on our cheeks, as we promised to be faithful to each other until we met again in Chicago. There were no sparkles in our eyes or smiles on our lips. Hoping the time would come when we would never part again. Such dreamers!

Zdenka and Olda

After my return home to Chicago, his letters kept coming and I answered them. There seemed to be not enough of them or often enough. I was getting tired of waiting, reading and writing, planning wishing and hoping, with no end in sight. He thought of leaving the country illegally as many of his friends had done, but it would have put his family in jeopardy. His brothers would have been denied higher education, and his father, who was in the governmental employment, would have lost his position. He felt too much loyalty and responsibility toward his family to cause them any hardship.

I belonged to several Czech youth clubs, where most of my friends were couples. I was getting lonely, but, of course, I had made a promise. I participated in *Sokol* gymnastic exhibitions, the Moravian Cultural Society, the Young Immigrants Czech Club, and attended cultural Czech affairs. Life was pretty normal, but I was miserable. My life was work, home, waiting for and writing letters. I attended a church choir with my friend Frances, Her family owned a cottage by Sag Canal, and, after she met her future husband Nick, we'd all pile up into his jeep on Saturday afternoons and spent the weekend there with her brothers and their friend, Benny. We had fun and needed this simple entertainment in the country.

One of the places we would go was Riverview Park.

Comet - Coaster Ride - Riverview Park - Chicago, Illinois

Nick and Francis wedding 1950

I was the maid of honor. She and her sister had a dual wedding.

1950s Moravian Day in Chicago, Pilsen Park. Left to right: Miroslava Tesař (sister), Wife of a Czech Consular in Washington, D.C. Zdenka Tesař

PART SEVEN:
Marriage

Things changed somewhat after my family's arrival. We started doing family things together. Hence in January, the Legionnaire Club held an annual formal dance in a hall on Pulaski Road in Chicago, and since my dad was a legionnaire, the whole family attended. Because this was a formal dance, we girls were all dressed in long gowns, and the young men wore evening attire also. The young people usually sat together, apart from the parents. I chose not to join my friends, because my friend at that time and I had had a disagreement earlier. So instead joining in with our young crowd, I stayed seated with my parents and my sister.

When music started after a short intermission, people started to get up to dance. That's when I spotted two male strangers in the doorway,. They were not dressed appropriately for this formal dance, which was odd. When music started, one of them started to cross the hall in the direction of our table! I hoped he was not coming over to ask me to dance. As he came closer, I thought maybe he was going to ask my sister. But no, he asked me to dance. Then, after the dance, he walked me back to our table and sat down! It was awkward. My English was not that good, and he seemed to be an American, not Czech! As we tried to converse, in order for him to understand what I was trying to tell him, he asked me "to draw him a picture." I did not know that it was just an expression, so I asked him for a pencil and paper! He produced a match book cover, and I drew on it! I do not remember what, but later on we always laughed about it.

After the dance ended, he volunteered to take the whole family home in his car! Wow! That made an impression on my mother! We all piled in, and before we got out of the car, he asked me if he could come over the next day, Sunday and take me out. Mother said it was OK.

The next day after Sunday dinner, we were all anxiously waiting for his arrival. He arrived in a blue Chevy. Mother noticed that he had a rip in his overcoat, which did not sit well with her. He came in and Father had a nice talk with him. They talked about the world and John's time spent in Australia, when he served in WW2. Then it was time to go on our date. But just then my mother decided, "Oh, NO, you are not going with him alone, you are taking your sister along! After all, we do not know him, where he comes from, and it just was not safe nor proper." So, the three of us went on our date. We went to the Douglas Park Conservatory, and it was very nice, but as those places go, it was very humid inside. By the time we left, my hair was wet and limp and I looked like a drowned mouse! So this started our courtship. We did not have a phone in the house, and I remember I was calling him from a phone booth on the way to my *Sokol* gym. By April 2nd, we were engaged. I felt alive again getting the attention I was craving.

On that evening, we went to a dance hall in McHenry, and he gave me a white camellia corsage and the engagement ring. Since the evening started on April Fools' Day we waited until midnight to get engaged. Of course he had to ask my parents for permission to marry me, even though I was 23 years old! I remember Mother warning him that I did not know how to cook, and Father apologizing for not being able to give me a dowry because they left it all in Czechoslovakia. The wedding was planned. I designed my wedding gown of white satin and arranged to have it sewn by a friend of Frances, the same lady that made Frances' wedding dress. We were married on September 30, 1950 in a little Bohemian Methodist church in the neighborhood where the Bank I worked for was located. We tried to get married in a Roman Catholic Church, even though John was not of that faith, but the priest wanted John to sign papers saying if I died, the children were to be brought up in Roman Catholic faith. That did not sound right to me and neither to John. I shared this with a co-worker at the bank and she made arrangements for us to talk with a young pastor in the neighborhood Methodist church. We did and liked him right away. He gave us our first Bible! My girlfriend, Frances, was to be my bridesmaid, but, because she was Roman Catholic, she was not allowed to! She wanted at least to attend my wedding, but that meant she would have to have gone into a protestant church which she was not allowed to do either. This is where her mother stepped in and said, "She is your best girlfriend. You go to the wedding!" And she did with her husband, Nick, forbidden or not!!!!

John insisted that I quit working after we married unless I could find an apartment near my work and not have to take public transportation. I found one! A coworker's family owned an apartment building in the neighborhood. We lived on the second floor and the rent was $ 17.00 a month. Part of the rent was that I had to wash the hallway stairs every other week. I was instructed to lay newspaper on the landings after the washing to help it to dry. We did not have a bathtub. There was only a toilet closet, so we had to walk to the nearby park to take public showers there! We had an oil heating stove in the living room to heat the apartment. We would haul the heating oil in a 5 gallon can every day to our 2nd floor apartment. We did not have a TV, just a radio/phonograph. We would lie on the floor to listen to the "Inner Sanctum Mysteries" radio program. One Sunday, we purchased a carpet on Maxwell Street, an outdoor market in the inner city, but I would not let John carry the carpet into the apartment because it was SUNDAY! To which he argued that we did not steal it, but bought it! Those days most of the stores were closed on Sundays. I did not feel right shopping on Sunday. It was also my first time dealing with wallpapering. I decided to wallpaper the kitchen with an ivy pattern. During that project, we nearly got a divorce!

By marrying John, I gained a new family since all my relatives were left behind in Czechoslovakia. I gained two sisters and a brother along with their spouses and children. Celebrating holidays would no longer have to be just with my own immediate family. There were, of course, some new customs to learn.

My cooking and baking had to be re-learned. My girlfriend, Frances, had bought me a Betty Crocker Cookbook as a wedding present. The bank was closed on Wednesdays, so this was my day to wash clothes and learn how to cook American-style. One Wednesday, I decided that I was going to make a pie with my new cookbook in hand. John had mentioned that he liked pumpkin pie. When he came home from work, I was so proud to show him my pie sitting in the center of the table. He asked me what kind of pie it was. I replied, "Pumpkin pie." And he exclaimed, "With a crust on top?"

Christmas holiday was fine, since my family celebrated on Christmas Eve and John's family gathered at their parents' home on Christmas Day. At first we used to gather at the Kiszkan family home on Parkside in Chicago, the Clearing neighborhood. In later years, we all got together at Ann and Stanley's home in Oak Forest, Illinois, in the suburbs of Chicago. There was always Santa with a sack of presents, which was new to me because Baby Jesus brought our presents in Czechoslovakia.

Also the Thanksgiving celebration was a new holiday for me. We celebrated harvest in the early fall or late summer with special recognition of the farmers and a special service at the church. We dressed in our national costumes and presented a special harvest wreath to a chosen farmer couple. In the afternoon there was a dance. Roasted turkey was also a novelty, not many people raised turkeys in Czechoslovakia it was rather a hand fed goose that was the queen of the holiday table.

1952 Light Blue Plymouth that we purchased new for $1300 cash.

In the winter, we used to put chairs in our shoveled-out parking space so that no one else would park there. I remember that John used to take the battery out of the car and put it behind the space heater in the living room to help the car to start in the morning.

My migraine headaches were happening more frequently and our hopes for getting pregnant were futile. I was so jealous of my girlfriend, Frances, because she already had two babies and we had both married the same year!

The rooming house 2234 S. Keeler, Chicago

We started to look for a house with my parents' help and found one. It was a big nine-room bungalow not far from them. We paid $ 13,800 which was a reasonable price for that time. John converted the upstairs four rooms into an apartment. His boss needed a place to live because the building where he had been renting had been sold. We still had the downstairs kitchen, the dining room, the living room and a bedroom. Later on we had a bedroom added on for the children. It was good. Our tenants had a little girl, Cathy, a delightful child. When the husband was transferred out of the state, we remodeled again and converted the upstairs into two single studio apartments and one two-room apartment. We were now in the rooming house business! Now I had a job, cleaning the hallway and stairs, and staying home taking care of my babies. Yes, we finally had a family.

We consulted our Doctor Gecht concerning our infertility. He instructed me to take a temperature reading every day to calculate the time of ovulation. Soon, we were expecting! My girlfriend, Frances, gave me the famous book by Dr. Spock to prepare me for pregnancy and delivery. I had a difficult pregnancy and spent the last month laying down. The doctor assured us that he had not lost a father yet! Finally, on a Saturday, things started to happen! We had a wild ride to the Illinois Masonic Hospital on the north side of Chicago. Being Saturday, there was not much work traffic, but John still went through every red traffic light anyway. It was probably the only time that he would have been able to talk his way out of a speeding ticket, but no police stopped us. Our son, John

Daniel, was born on May 28.1955 at 2:00 p.m. We were parents!!! He was one week early, which was OK with me.

Proud parents with baby John Daniel

1955

Our daughter Gloria Ann was born only 16 months later. I was delighted to have a girl this time. I was ready for one because, before our son was born, I had sewn a christening gown using left over white satin material from my wedding gown and sporting a BONNET! Poor little Johnny had to wear it with just a minor alternation. I put blue ribbons on the bonnet!!! Gloria was born on Sunday September 30 1956, exactly at 11:00 a.m. Just the time of Sunday worship time! Therefore her name just HAD to be Gloria, praising God for this gift.

Zdenka and Gloria

1956 Gloria's Christening

Somehow we got into raising parakeets, another business venture. John installed large flight cages in the basement, and we learned how to raise these birds. The wall was lined with nesting boxes. Do you know that the birds will not mate until they are in those nesting boxes? Sometimes, they have more brains then people! We sold the parakeets to local pet shops.

In the meantime, my sister met a fellow at one of the Bohemian clubs and got married. I was the maid of honor and made the wedding cake. My sister worked at the Land O' Lakes Creamery and Bohumil was an electrician. They lived in an apartment for a while, then purchased an apartment building in Berwyn. Bohous turned the basement into a laundromat. They had one son, Milan.

1960 Miroslava & Bohumil Kratky wedding

Our family made many trips to Michigan. Our first trip was in 1956 to establish the location of the property given to us by my father via Anna Misar, his school friend. My husband, John, our son, Johnny, Mother and Father with Mrs. Misar took on this adventure. I stayed home with our new baby, Gloria. Locating the property turned out to be quite an adventure. After several false leads, John decided to stop at a local tavern, the Hiltop, to get something to drink. There were no other eating establishments in Holton at that time. There the "investigating" group met Mr. Bartoszek who was willing to show them the property since he was a long-time Holton resident. Finally the vision became a reality. Of course, Mrs. Anna Misar did not believe that it was the right spot. She "remembered" that there was a field of onions on it when her and her husband purchased the property 20 years ago! I guess, time just flies by too quickly and the onions did not survive the time!

As a family, we spent our first vacation close to OUR property. We rented a cottage in Twin Lake at Zimmerman cottages. The following year we "roughed it" sleeping in our Ford Station Wagon and cooking outdoors on a makeshift fireplace!. The kids enjoyed the Twin Lake Park and learning how to swim. When one of our neighbors' small mobile home was damaged by fire, we purchased it. With the help of our other neighbors, the Ingrams, we hauled the damaged trailer on to our property. This became our vacation home for many years, and we enjoyed painting it and making it more livable every year. It was an improvement, from the station wagon arrangements.

Later, Johnny became a Boy Scout and attended the Camp Owassippi nearby for one week every summer. We would then spend another week at OUR camp site together! Johnny and Gloria always enjoyed playing with the neighbor kids, the Ingrams.

One summer, when Ann (John's sister) and her husband, Stanley, came to visit, we installed a water pump! Roy Ingram, our neighbor, built us an "instrument" for digging: two 2x4s attached to a stump, we took turns to pound the ground with it. There was a well "tip" at the bottom of the stump with an extending pipe and somehow we reached WATER!!!!! We purchased a small hand pump and we were in business!!! What a joy to be able to pump our own water! We all took turns washing our faces and grinning ear to ear! What an accomplishment!!!

Our new pump did not last. The following summer, our vacation trailer was broken into and the pump also disappeared! So, it was back to hauling water from the previous site of our burned out trailer. My sister Miroslava (Myra) and her husband Bohumil Kratky, purchased the little property where the trailer had once stood and the operating pump was still there. There was a new house trailer on the property, that belonged to our old neighbors Barbahans, from Worth, Illinois. Our children and their friends learned how to drive the old station wagon through the woods, not ON the road, to get water. They did not mind this chore a bit!

We picked blueberries, searched the sand dunes across the road for Indian arrowheads and pretty stones, picked mushrooms, had bonfires, and roasted marshmallows. No schedules. Just good, simple life.

Back at home, another move loomed over our heads. John's company had relocated to the suburbs of Chicago and traveling became an issue. This time, we purchased a home in the town of Worth, Illinois. It was a brand new home ,but not quite finished as far as the inside decorating. No problem. John's sister, Ann, got a crew together (her two boys, me, and her) and we painted all the rooms. I started in the closets, which was her method of teaching someone how to paint! Johnny was by now about 2 years old and Gloria was 8 months old. The yard needed lots of work: a lawn had to be put in and I was going to have a .little garden in the back .The back yard was kind of swampy. We later discovered that it was more of a sewage problem. John helped me to build flower beds around the house using flag stone.

The children started school in our town of Worth, Illinois. They were able to walk to school. I then decided to enter the work force again and got a job at a local Norge Laundromat where Ann, my sister-in-law, worked. It was walking distance from our house, and I was able to be home when the children returned home from school

I joined the PTA and we joined the Worth Methodist Church, where the children started Sunday school. I also joined the choir and the WSCS, a women's organization. I helped with the Vacation Bible School at the church in the summers. As the children grew, I became a Camp Fire Girls leader sponsored by the church. John became a Weblo leader for the Boys scouts, which was also sponsored by the church. Life was good, until one day my husband came home from work and announced that he had purchased a grocery store business with living quarters and we were moving back to Chicago!!!!

Family photo 1970

After the shock wore off, many arrangements needed to be made. Since John still worked at the Sherwin-Williams plant in south Chicago, I was delegated to run the business. My mother graciously came to our home and took care of the children. The entire family got together on weekends in Chicago. We sold our Worth home and made the final move after Christmas. The children had to transfer to new schools and we joined the Elsdon Methodist church. There were two Sunday services at the church which enabled us to take turns attending church and watching the store. My husband went to the first service with one of the children, and I went to the second service with the other child.

The store was open seven days a week with shorter hours on Sunday. With the toll of the constant attention required by the business, our family started to fall apart. In order to get some relaxation, we divided our times with the children. One Sunday I would take our son, John, to spend the afternoon away from the store. The next Sunday, John would take Gloria and go bowling or some other fun activity. Later on, we decided to close the store on Sunday afternoons, so that we could spent time together as a family. We finally sold the business and bought a Cape Cod style home in the same school district. With some of the profits from the business, we decided to visit Czechoslovakia. Johnny loved the idea right away, but Gloria was hesitant. She wanted to stay with my mother but we eventually forced her to go. It was 1972-3. I'm not quite sure of the year. We stayed with my uncle, Julius Tabery, in Prague for few days, and then continued to my home town of Korycany in Moravia. We rented Fiat at the Ruzyne Airport in Prague. We had lots of "fun" driving in Prague, where we also received our first TICKET. Uncle Julius only used street cars for transportation and was not familiar with driving rules. I wanted my family to see where I spent 17 years of my life and where I received my first formal education. It was fun and rewarding. We spent a few days in Vienna, Austria. The kids went on a disco tour while John and I took a more leisurely guided night tour.

Uncle Julius

Then we continued south to Lake Wortasees where we went fishing on a little motor-run boat, visited Salzburg (from the Sound of Music), visited the Mozart summer home, and took a ride thru the Alps and the peak, Glockenheimer. Scary! The tip of the mountain had a tunnel with no end in sight, it was really that high up in the clouds. But with determination and also with no other alternative, we made it.

We arrived in Italy, where we made it as far as Venice. There we took a gondola ride, fed the pigeons on St Mark square, visited Murano glass works, stayed on the Italian Riviera at a Pension Hotel for few days and decided to head back to Czechoslovakia. The August summer heat was too hard to take.

When we arrived back in Prague, turned our rental car in at the Ruzyne Airport and decided not to stay with Uncle Julius, because his apartment was just too small. We picked a hotel about 30 km west of Prague in town of Slany to finish our remaining days of vacation time. After checking in,at the hotel Slany, the receptionist was surprised that we were from USA. The manager of the hotel, Mr, Jan Cermak, introduced himself to us and wanted us to meet friends of his whose mother was from United States. It was a pleasant meeting and we became friends for life. Thus was a beginning of a life-long friendship. Funny, how God puts people into our lives.

1974 Art Fair

Back home in Chicago, I began taking evening art classes at Hubbard High School which I enjoyed greatly. The teacher, Mr. Shrey, was a former art teacher of Gloria's from the time when she was a student at HHS. I eventually wound up with a large number of paintings. For several years, I exhibited at neighborhood art fairs and even managed to sell a few!

Now, my parents were getting older, and my father eventually passed on in 1976. It became more worrisome taking care of mother. She insisted on living in their home. "What would Father say, if she moved?" she queried. Many times, when we called her in the evening, there was no answer, so we would have to drive to her house to make sure that she was OK. She was always fine; she just had not heard the phone!

U.S., Social Security Death Index, 1935-2014 about John Tesař

Name:	**John Tesař**
SSN:	326-28-4633
Last Residence:	60623 Chicago, Cook, Illinois, USA
BORN:	13 Sep 1883
Died:	Mar 1976
State (Year) SSN issued:	Illinois (1951)

When her downstairs tenant died leaving that apartment vacant, we made a decision. Johnny was living in his first apartment and Gloria was away at college, so we sold our house and moved into Mother's building in the empty downstairs apartment. It was easier to keep an eye on her. We were able to monitor her health and were sure that she had her meals with us.

My mother and I in the choir at Elsdon United Methodist Church in Chicago in 1976. My mom is 1st from the right in the second row and I am behind her, second from right.

I was working part-time at Sears, because of Gloria On her Christmas college break, she decided to get a little job there and I got signed up for a job, too. I stayed with the company almost 11 years, always expecting to be laid off since I was originally only Christmas help!

On another one of Gloria's college breaks, I started to attend Daley College. When Gloria had come home, she registered at Daley College to earn some college credit over the summer. She asked me to go with her, and while there suggested that I sign up for an art class. I was apprehensive about what my husband would say, but Gloria offered to call him and get his approval. So I became a student and eventually graduated in 1981 with a degree in Art. Of course, I had to take several other classes, like Chemistry, Oceanography, Biology, and etc. in order to fulfill the requirements for graduating!

My college graduation

But, I am getting ahead of myself.

Johnny graduated from Hubbard High School in Chicago but did not want to go to college. At first, he wanted to join the military instead of finishing high school. We agreed that he could join the military but only AFTER he finished high school. These plans did not materialize, and after graduating, Johnny got a job at a mattress factory and moved into an apartment with a friend. After his friend moved out, John kept the apartment and invited us one evening for a dinner that he had prepared himself! I knew he planned on making a meat loaf from the phone calls he had made to our house all day long! That's when I bought him a cookbook entitled, *How to Cook Ground Beef 100 Different Ways*. By the way, the dinner was very good.

Gloria graduated from YMCA Central High School in the year 1973. She had dropped out of Hubbard High School and then managed to accomplish her last two years of schooling in one year at YMCA Central and graduated with honors. She originally did not want to continue her education but later changed her mind and was accepted at North Central College in Naperville.

After one year at North Central College, a private school, Gloria ran out of college savings and then applied to a Western Illinois University in Macomb, Illinois. She majored in Psychology and graduated college with honors before her 19th birthday! She got involved in women's issues there, and eventually moved off campus and rented a cottage .She had a garden and grew much of the food that she lived on!

Gloria's college graduation

Gloria's first job after graduating was at an employment agency in Chicago. She soon got an apartment with a friend from college, and I was sad that another of my children was leaving the nest. Gloria assured me not to worry because she would come home every Monday evening for supper as Johnny was doing! This was also his "laundry time" at our house! Gloria became disillusioned with the clients at the employment office not following through on leads and appointments and making it very hard to earn any money.

She then worked for a year as a clerk at Levinson's Jewelry in Chicago. After a disagreement with her boss, she got fired and earned her living for some time painting, plastering and cleaning houses. This work gave her the flexibility to take her time finding her next job.

On the advice on her brother, who was now working at ConRail Railroad, Gloria applied for a job with the Chicago, Milwaukee, St. Paul, and Pacific Railroad Company. After 6 weeks of training classes, she began work by filling in for employees who were on vacation. Eventually she landed a permanent job as a clerk, and was later promoted to Station Agent. After the CMSTP&P declared bankruptcy, they scaled down their workforce and Gloria spent the rest of her railroad career working as a control operator.

By this time she had purchased her first house in Round Lake Park, a suburb of Chicago, closer to her job. She had a roommate, also a railroad employee, who helped with expenses.

Back at home, John and I began to plan our retirement and decided to build a home on our Michigan property. By 1971, we had a beginning of a house. Ed Murat with his son-in-law Fred Ingram, built the foundation for our home. First the cement floor was poured and then the cement block walls went up. We purchased windows from the Muskegon Building Company. Now we had, what they called a "Michigan basement house!" This served us for several years, but it had, of course, a flat roof. Anytime we arrived, we had to literally "shovel" water from the inside of the house. The flat roof was leaking!!! There was only a cement floor, so nothing got really hurt, but it became obvious that we needed to do something and soon.

Michigan "basement house"

Looking for a builder became a problem, since we lived in Chicago, Illinois and the house was in Michigan. Most of the builders in Michigan had their own construction sites to build on. They also built houses with one design only. As we stopped at different building sites, one of the builders suggested Paul Johnson, who was a custom house builder. After we located him, we presented him with our "plans." I had seen a house in one of the catalogs and with some minor alterations, decided, that was the house we wanted .Paul Johnson lived on Bard Rd, near M120 and had built his own home. We were anxious to get the building going and he was willing to build it.

We agreed to have him put up a shell of the house, with windows and doors installed with double glass and screens. We used to come for the weekends to work on the interior of the house. As for a floor plan, I just drew on the top of the flat roof, where the rooms should be, but he had to make some changes.

Back of completed house in the winter

Completed house 2013

John and I went to Hawaii for our 25th anniversary in 1975.

1925   1975
The Children of
Mr. and Mrs. John Tesar
request the honour of your presence
at the
Fiftieth Wedding Anniversary
of their parents
Sunday, the eighteenth of May
nineteen hundred and seventy-five
Elsdon United Methodist Church
5300 South Christiana Avenue
at ten-thirty in the morning
Reception
at two o'clock in the afternoon
Moravian House
4142 West 26th Street
Chicago, Illinois

My parents' 50th wedding anniversary was also in 1975. We celebrated with a ceremony at Elsdon United Methodist Church in Chicago and a party after at the Moravian House. Uncle Julius was able to join the festivities coming in from Czechoslovakia.

We went to Peru with Gloria and Johnny in 1978. There was a Peruvian Exhibit at this time at the Chicago Museum, and at the same time, they were advertising trips to Peru. John and I decided to go. Johnny and Gloria were also interested so we invited them along. So much "living on their own!"

Then John and I went to St Croix with Barb and Melvin in 1979. We went to Martinique with Gloria Melvin, and Barb the next year. And to Cancun, Mexico with Gloria and Heather in 1985. There we took a trip to Chichen-Itza, the Mayan ruins, where we lost Heather, but found her later. She just got turned around and missed the bus.

By the time we made our permanent move to Michigan in 1983, the house was finished. It took us several months to do the inside finishing, since we were able to come up for weekends. We had electricity in the house, and we stayed in the unfinished downstairs when we came up. That was also another great improvement, having one light bulb in the main room with a socket for an electric frying pan! We were "living it up!" We decided on paneling the walls upstairs in the living room and kitchen to have them maintenance free. Only the two upstairs bedrooms would be not paneled. John did all the plumbing and electrical work. He used the Chicago codes for proper installation. Our kitchen cabinets were purchased at Sears in Chicago and hauled by John as were all the other necessary items to finish the house. When we put the bats of insulation between the studs, it looked so grand that I called it the Silver Palace! Then all the light fixtures were put in place. For heating we had a little woodstove upstairs which kept us reasonably warm. Later Paul Johnson's brother installed a wood/oil furnace, it was a special order from Missouri, so that was another great advance toward our goal to move in.

Early in the year of 1982, John was laid off from Sherwin-Williams Company in Chicago. He was close to his retirement, so our move to Michigan became a reality. We started earnestly packing, and John made weekly trips to Michigan to unload and continued working on finishing the house. We planned on bringing my mother, Beata Tesař, with us.

First I had asked my sister if she would have liked to have Mom live with her. I thought Mom would have been more comfortable there, keeping in touch with her friends and would be some help with Milly's son, Milan, my nephew. He was still in school, and there would have been someone to take care of him after school. My sister was now alone, having been separated from her husband. She worked as a domestic health care giver. I did not feel that Mother should be left alone in the house in Chicago. But my sister felt it was the duty of the oldest child to take care the parents, and so it was decided that we would take Mother with us to Michigan.

I did not think that the move would be a problem for Mom. She knew our house in Michigan, the neighbors, etc., because we brought her with us anytime we traveled there. She always enjoyed it in Michigan. However, after we moved, we began to notice that Mother was showing signs of Alzheimer's. In retrospect, all the signs had been there in Chicago, we just didn't want to see them: She would lock herself out of the house and either spent time with neighbors or had someone using a ladder climb into the house to open the door.. Of course, when I got home from work, she was already either IN the house, or rang the doorbell to come back home saying she was visiting neighbors and forgot to take her keys!

We originally hoped, that she would be living separate from us in the downstairs quarters to give her privacy. The downstairs was completely finished with a full kitchen, a bathroom, a bedroom, and a full living room with a fireplace. We even installed a garden window so that she could keep her plants that she loved. But this was not going to be. She refused to live downstairs, and so we settled her into one of the bedrooms upstairs. We furnished her bedroom with her own bed, her own television set, and pictures of Dad on the walls to make her feel more at home. She seemed to be happy.

I kept on working at Sears in Muskegon until one day when John told me he had enough of taking care of my mother while I was not at home. After all, she was MY mother! Luckily an opportunity presented itself. The Muskegon Mall was being demolished and the Sears store where I had been working was being relocated. I was offered a position at the Grand Rapids Sears store, but the daily drive was not up to my liking. Instead, I took a retirement package with benefits and severance pay.

When we moved to Michigan, I joined the United Methodist church in Holton. Every Sunday, Mother and I went to church services. We invited John to come with us, but he always had an excuse: too much work! One Sunday, we were shocked when he got dressed in a suit and drove to the church with us!. Later on, we joined the senior citizens' group at the church, and I joined the choir. John made some special friends, Carl Dake and Bill Reno. It was Bill and his wife Pat that helped us to get acquainted with the state of Michigan. We took Sunday drives and once took the train thru the Upper Peninsula and Canada. We also took several winter vacations together in Gulf Shores, Alabama.

John and I went to the Holy Land in 1988 combined with Jordan and Egypt with twelve members of Holton United Methodist Church and our Pastor David McBride and his wife Bonnie. That was a very memorable trip. As John commented later, that trip really brought the Bible ALIVE!

Mt. NEBO, JORDAN

Our life in Michigan was a lot different than in Chicago. John wanted to be a gentlemen farmer. The life had a different routine. He bought a pickup truck, built fences, and he kept several pigs. He also loved his geese; he called them his "girls," and took them for walks around the property. At one time we had some sheep, including an old male we called Ali Baba. We also had chickens and he raised some big ones. We even purchased a feather stripper machine! We could butcher, pluck and dress a chicken in 7 minutes! I loved irises and John purchased a whole field of them for me which we planted behind the house. They replaced the huge vegetable garden that we had there before. I was "done" with canning! Our friends' and family's visits became less frequent.

Our son John was married on May 1, 1981in Chicago .

Not only did we gain a daughter-in-law, but we gained a granddaughter as well.
Heather was the child of Sheryl from her previous marriage. We were delighted with the little cutie; she was only just over one year old. We assumed the new role of grandparents quickly. It was a lovely wedding with favors of ceramic heart shape boxes made by Sheryl. Most of the family were able to attend. They were married at Elsdon UMC in Chicago, Illinois.

They had already purchased a home on Sawyer Street and Kedzie Avenue, Chicago Illinois. Sheryl's mother, Stella Hope, and Sheryl's sister, Holly, were to live in the upstairs apartment. John and Sheryl met while working at Conrail Railroad. Sheryl's father, Tom Hope, had been a long-time railroad man. Johnny did remodeling inside, and he had now a yard to take care of. They purchased large above ground swimming pool and it was used a lot.

About 4 years later, Heather was so excited to tell us, that she was going to have a new brother or sister! Our first grandson was born on July 25, 1985 and was named David John. I remember that Auntie Ann (John's sister) would sometimes call him

Johnny to which David would reply, "It's OK, my middle name is JOHN!" He had red hair, probably because of the genes of Sheryl's father. Auntie Ann loved David's red hair and always teased him that he should let her have that hair!! Another addition to Johnny and Sheryl's family came on September 28. 1987. This time it was a little girl named Sheri Nicole. The middle name came as part of the Ukrainian heritage.

Gloria met her future husband, Tony (Lucien Alphonse) Charland, Jr. at the railroad. He had twin boys from his first marriage who lived with their mother in Wisconsin. By this time Gloria owned several rental homes, and Tony and she moved to her lake house in Ingleside because Tony had a boat.

They got married on March 18. 1989, in Long Grove Village, Illinois, a quaint, historical town. Our long -time friend, Pastor Tom Hendrix, came in from Springfield, Illinois to do the ceremony. It was fitting since he had known Gloria from her childhood. I made the cake for the wedding which everyone enjoyed. It was a very special day.

Back in Michigan, my mom enjoyed the animals on our little farm and seemed to be happy, but the Alzheimer's was taking her life away. She loved to watch John on the tractor that was something new to her. She liked to see our "visitors," the deer We fed them apples, carrots and sugar beets. She also liked to feed the different birds. We would record cassettes to mail to her brother Julius in Prague because writing became too difficult for her. After the doctor confirmed her illness it became more and more difficult to take care of her. By now she required 24 hour care and his reasoning was that we were not trained for that. There was a Foster Care Adult Home in our town that we were able to secure a place for her there. It was just five minutes from our house, so it was very convenient. However, as time went on, her body deteriorated to the point that she had to be transferred into a nursing home in Muskegon. Not long after that though, the diagnosis were grim and it was suggested by the nursing home, that we take her home to die surrounded by the family.

Mother passed away on September 27, 1991 at the age of 95 in Holton, Michigan. We had the funeral rites at our church in Holton with a little funeral luncheon prepared by the ladies of Holton United Methodist Church. Her body was later transported to Chicago for the final rites at Svec Funeral Home in Berwyn on October 2, 1991. She was well-known in the Czech community there and it gave her friends a chance to say good-bye. Her ashes were interred at the Bohemian National Cemetery in Chicago in the same niche as her husband, John (Jan).

My sister, Miroslava (Myra) Kratky passed away the following spring in 1992. I received the news of her passing while I was on a trip to Washington D,C. She had been a widow for 14 years since her estranged husband, Bohumil Kratky, had passed away in 1978 from a brain tumor. Enough of these sad memories.

In the summer of 1992 Margaret Charland, Tony's mother, and I flew to the Czech Republic where we researched some of the places of her mother and relatives. That was a very interesting trip. We were able to locate the cemetery where her grandmother was buried and the church that she was married in.

After some time Gloria and Tony were finally blessed with a son, Lucien Alphonse III, on December 18, 1992. After some time had passed, they wanted another child and decided to adopt. This time the baby girl came by adoption from St. Petersburg,

Russia. In March of 1996, we brought tiny little Ekaterina home to the USA. She was born on July 18, 1995. I was privileged to travel to Russia with them to bring her home.

The adoption agency had sent a video of her and all of us fell in love! The weather was gloomy when we arrived in St. Petersburg airport and we were housed in the apartment of a retired woman who was subletting her apartment to adoptive families. The next day we were taken by a cab to the St. Petersburg orphanage which was located of outside the city. It was a rundown cab, and the tire wells rubbed on the tires because of the load of passengers. I wondered if the car would make it to the destination! The trip took over an hour through the snowy, dismal countryside, dotted with small frame houses, painted with dark colors surrounded with broken down fences. We never saw any people; it was probably too cold. Finally we arrived at a large building with several floors, quite different from the ones we encountered along the way. There was even a small yard with some playground equipment. The reception room was quite nice with a pleasant lady, the director. After some formalities, a nurse brought in the little star - Ekaterina!

She was full of smiles especially when Lucien was performing somersaults for her! We all held her and talked to her, what joy! Gloria came prepared with baby clothes, diapers and formulas and after she re-dressed her, we were on our way to Moscow. I wanted to take a picture of Ekaterina's room, but was told that they were "remodeling" so it was not possible.

In Moscow we were again housed in a private home and spent the day running around trying to get Ekaterina's passport and visa. It was Saturday and not many places were opened. We had time to visit church services, it was Russian Easter. The next day we went to the Red Square, St. Basil Cathedral, Lenin's Tomb and later tried to go to a flea market, but it was raining. We even found McDonalds!

Back home, John had started to show signs of Parkinson's disease as early as 1992. We were all baffled by his behavior, his inability to function and after being definitely diagnosed with the illness, our life changed. Neurologist visits, surgeries, rehabilitation, home care, and over and over again, until in 1999, the doctors refused to let him come home from the hospital and he entered a nursing home in Fremont. At this time, he was experiencing TIAs, small strokes, was not able to walk at all, he spent all his time in a wheel chair. He lost his sense of reality.

In May of 1999, with John safely in a nursing home, I was able to get away for a mental health break as recommended by John's doctors. I flew to the Czech Republic. I stayed with the Kotva family, who picked me up at the airport. It was a happy time. We drove to my home town Korycany and visited my old home. There were new owners, but they were gracious enough, to let me roam through the house. They did some remodeling to suit their life style. Later, after returning to Kladno, we went to visit their summer cottage several miles away. We also connected with Eva, my Uncle Julius' friend for many years. We attended an opera house in Prague and saw a play by Kafka, The Metamorphosis, We also went to see another play, something modern, at another theater in Prague, but I do not recall the name. We visited some gardens and walked up to the Castle, the Czech Governmental offices and St. Vitus Cathedral. My stay was short I believe only about two weeks. Back home, refreshed, I felt ready to face the reality of life

There were times that John did not know who I was and he spoke less and less. It became more difficult for him to swallow food. He passed away that year on October 24 after being at the home for only seven months. His body was cremated, and the burial of his ashes took place the following May of 2000. The ashes of his beloved dog, Gypsy, were buried with him. John earned the honors to be buried in a special Veteran Section because of his service in the Navy, during the WW2.

Also in 1999, we lost John's sister, Ann Peters, and, about a month later, her husband, Stanley.

In July of that same year, I lost my nephew, Milan, my sister Myra's son. He was only in his 30s when he passed on very unexpectedly. He lived in his mother's home, after she passed on and was doing some remodeling on the apartments. One weekend, he felt ill and, thinking he had the flu, went to the hospital, where they told him to go home and drink plenty of fluids. He did not have any insurance, so this was their diagnosis. His roommate called us the next day, Sunday, to tell us that he found Milan on the kitchen floor and he had an ambulance transfer him to the hospital. He was in a coma and there was no chance for recovery. To keep him alive he would be like a "vegetable" They recommend to "pull the plug" When we arrived at the hospital from Michigan on Monday, that's what we were told. At this time I was approached by a team of nurses, if I would be willing to donate some of his organs. It was a hard decision, but if Milan was put on this earth for a purpose, this might have been the one. In losing his life, he enabled another to gain it. I performed the funeral service and his ashes were interred near his parents in the Bohemian Cemetery in Chicago, Illinois.

Milan Kratky

PART SEVEN:
Widowhood

Thus my life took on a different meaning and style: widowhood, and with it came many changes. I was still busy at church which gave me a great deal of fulfillment. I belonged to a Bible study group, the church choir, and was a member in UMW (United Methodist Women). I started taking exercise classes again and learned to make many decisions on my own. I was glad that I knew how to drive so I could to visit my children and the grandchildren. I loved to travel and made many trips abroad. Thanks to my daughter, Gloria, I was able to visit many countries. I am grateful to her for dragging me along and putting up with me.

One of my first trips with Gloria's family was to the state of Washington in 2001 to attend Tony's son, Scott's, wedding. We made many stops along the way: the Black Hills of South Dakota, Mount *Rushmore*, and a Czech museum in Cedar Rapids, Iowa. We also visited Tony's sister in Idaho and saw the Oregon Trail. I had never even heard of the Oregon Trail, so this was an interesting history lesson for me. The museum was awesome, with several scenes of the courageous journey to the West by the first pioneer settlers. Finally, we arrived at Olympia, Washington. Of course, the wedding was lovely.

Also in 2001, I took my granddaughter, Sheri, to the Czech Republic in the mid-summer. She was bored and I do not blame her much. She spent of her time hanging out with us "old folks." She did enjoy some of her experiences, and later on, enjoyed that she had seen some of the places that she was studying in school the next year.

My first trip to Guatemala was with Gloria and her family. She collected several cases of baby clothes which we took to a hospital in Jocotenango. These were welcomed and given to the new mothers that came from the mountains. Some of the indigenous mothers were so poor that they had no clothing in which to dress their newborn babies nor blankets to wrap them in when they left the hospital.

We returned again in November of that same year to attend the wedding of our Guatemalan friends, Luis and Marisol. There was another new experience for me, witnessing a wedding ceremony that included ancient Mayan rituals. While at the church during the wedding rites, I had an unusual feeling and could not put my finger on it.

Something was just not right! As I looked around, I noticed that most of the attendees were shorter than me! Even though I was 5'2 I towered over them!

In 2002 I went to Boston with Gloria's family and learned a lot that I had never known about American history. I never had the opportunity before, and it was just wonderful. We walked the streets of Boston, following the "red brick" path on the sidewalks. We visited several historical homes of early prominent citizens and I learned about some little known facts. For instance; when an artist was commissioned to paint a portrait, it had to be decided, if the portrait will include an arm or a leg in the painting, since the cost of the portrait would be then higher. Therefore the saying "it will cost you an arm and a leg" Also, to profess their Christian beliefs, it became a custom of incorporating a cross on their doors. Next time you see a door, look for that cross, it is there! There was another interesting tidbit about the saying, " Dead as a door nail." Because of the open fireplaces in homes, many homes burned down. The nails were collected from the rubble and used to rebuilt the homes, but some nails were saved to be pound in the entry door, in memory of lives lost during that fire. One per each person.

Our visit to the East Coast would not have been complete without stopping in Salem, where the trials of witches were held. We attended a live presentation of the recreation of one of the well-known historical witch trials.

One year, Gloria's home school group had an international fair and I was asked to do a presentation on Czechoslovakia. We made a poster and I collected history on the country and shared my knowledge of the country. It was a wonderful experience. I guess once a Czech, always a Czech!

Throughout my life I have had many hobbies. Though I had always loved art, and painting and studying the great artists had been my passion, I found a new hobby later in life: stained glass artistry. I first studied this craft in Chicago and took to it whole-heartedly. I set up a small shop in our basement in the Michigan house and continued making pieces small and large after our move. However, the most rewarding stained glass work I ever accomplished was renovating two large stained glass windows from the old Holton United Methodist Church that were later installed on either side of the altar at the new Holton United Methodist Church building. Some friends helped and a talented parishioner made new lighted frames for them out of wood. I feel these are my legacy to leave to the future generations at the new church.

One memorable vacation I took was when Gloria, Lucien, Katie and I flew to Czechoslovakia. We made a three day stop in Amsterdam and stayed in a downtown hotel, so we were near the hub of all of the activities. We visited a wax museum on the Dam square. And we saw the palace. We even saw a ballet performance on the square. We found and toured the home of Ann Frank where her family hid from the Nazis. We had to stop the Van Gogh Museum to see some his original paintings and took a leisurely ride in a glass boat on the main canal. In Prague at the Ruzyn airport, we were met by my friends, Pavel and Jarka Kotva. Since my uncle Julius had passed on, they offered to share their home with us. Within a few days, Pavel drove us to my home town of Korycany. I had a chance to visit my old home and had a nice visit with my two of my schoolmates. I was able to show my grandchildren the school I attended as a child. After few days we returned back to Kladno, and my friend Jarka drove us to the city of Prague, where we visited some historical sites. The time flew by and soon we were ready to return to USA.

My first trip to Thailand was in 2004, where I fell in love with the people and the country and made some new friends. I had a chance to travel there with Judy, a friend from my church, whose granddaughter was there as an English teacher the previous year. We were joined by Judy's brother, Jim, and his wife, Barbara.

On my third trip to Antigua, Guatemala in 2005, I took my grandson, David, with us. It was his turn to travel with Grandma. We visited the ruins at Tikal and Lucien, Katie, and David climbed the stairs of one Mayan pyramid all the way to the top! David also attended a Spanish language school as Gloria and her children always did. I tried it on my first trip but gave up after that! Too much for this old brain! David was a delight to travel with.

In 2006, Gloria made arrangements to fly to Greece, the cradle of democracy. It was rich in history, which Lucien, Katie, Gloria and I just loved! Lucien even ran on the field where the Olympic Games were once held. Seeing the Acropolis was sight to be behold. To see Greece properly, one must take the cruise to visit the islands. What a reverent moment it was to stand on the ground of the island of Patmos, where St. John wrote the Book of Revelations. Also, we visited the island of Crete with the ruins of the Palace of Knossos. Our ship also stopped in Istanbul, Turkey. I marveled at the beautiful Blue Sophia Mosque, which was under renovation and of course, had to visit the spice bazaar which had more than just spices. Finally, we toured the main island of Greece with all the wonders there. I can truly say it was a "bucket list" trip!

I then visited the Czech Republic again in 2007 with my friend from church, Connie Zerlaut. During this visit, we took a bus trip to Hungary with Jarka Kotva and another friend from Prague, Eva.

In May of 2008, I flew to Panama for 3 weeks with Gloria, Lucien and Katie. Another country with new adventures! We explored Panama City and our cab driver took us one day to the native island of Sopora. Gloria, Lucien and Katie went ´zip lining" over the tree tops of the jungle. No thanks, not for me, I was the photographer! Gloria heard about an island only accessible by motor boat which had a sanctuary for Sea Turtles. They layed their eggs in the black sand beach. These were collected by volunteers and buried in a protected area to be watched over until the baby turtles hatched. It was a very interesting island and had no electricity! Combine the black sand with no electricity and patrolling at midnight, and the only way you can walk is by sheer instinct! After leaving Panama City we flew to the island of Boca de Toros and rented a cottage with bicycles for transportation! That's what Gloria Katie and Lucien used to get to Language School every day.

In 2009, I visited Guatemala again with Gloria's family and Lucien's friend, Nathan, This time we took a trip to see the ruins in Honduras. I saw beautiful Macau parrots flying freely through the trees. I learned about the cashew nut trees and, of course, roamed the grounds covered with Mayan ruins. The weather was wonderful and our guide was " Crazy." And I literally mean "crazy" with his funny hat adorned with feathers!

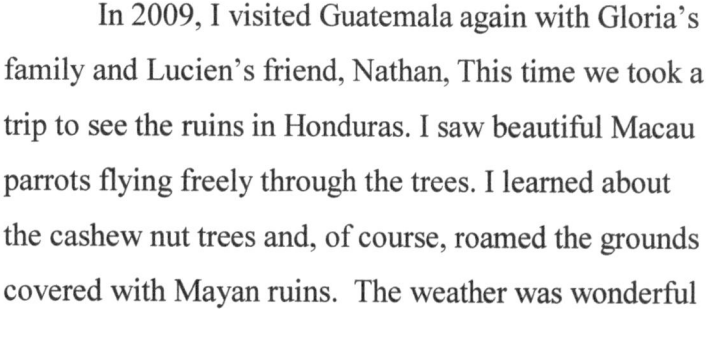

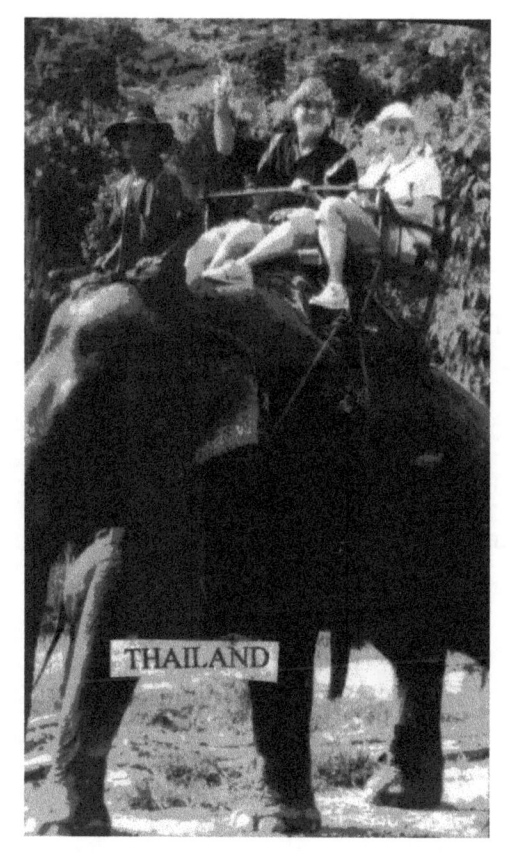

Also in 2009 I took my son Johnny to visit Thailand. It was a great trip with many aah's and ooh's .He loved the country as much as I do. Nong picked us up in Bangkok and took us to their home in Sawan Nakhon. We did lots of sightseeing saw some beautiful temples. Afterwards she drove us to a town where we rejoined our tour. We flew to the northern part of Thailand and John was able ride an elephant through the jungle. He very much enjoyed meeting my friend, Nong, and even visited their local school with her. It was a delightful time that we spent with her husband and children. On this trip, we met some new friends, Isabelle, Don and Louise, with whom we are still in touch today.

I believe it was in spring of 2010 that Johnny and I visited Czech Republic. He had not been there since 1973, when our family took a trip there. We stayed with my friends the Kotvas, and John had a wonderful time mushroom hunting wih Pavel. They were very successful! They brought back baskets full. We also visited my friend, Eva, in Prague and, after sightseeing, had dinner at her home. While there, she suggested very casually if I would like to meet with my friend, Olda? I had no idea that she had his phone number or that she knew of him! Well, my answer was of course "yes" and she got in touch with him. He came to Eva's home and we all had a pleasant dinner. I introduced him to my son, John, who, as usual, took many photographs. Olda surprised me when he handed me a pouch of letters. They were the ones that I wrote to him so many years ago/ He had them all numbered. There were over 56 of them! WOW! I had to confess to him that I burned all his letters after I married and had children .We reminisced on the 60 years since 1949. It was a nice visit. When I returned home to USA, we kept in touch for a while.

Then in 2011 Gloria scheduled a trip for us to Spain, where we stayed for three weeks. This time we had Nathan and his sister Mae, but no Lucien. They all attended Spanish Language school. We were housed in a private home in town of Malaga, right off the beach, where we spent many happy hours. We roamed the Picasso museum and saw many of his original paintings. I was surprised to see an ancient outdoor theater in Malaga built by the Romans.

Malaga, Spain

One weekend, we visited Morocco on the continent of Africa. On the way there we saw the Rock of Gibraltar.

Some rock! Gloria should have been a travel adviser! We also had a chance to visit some pre-historic caves with cave paintings! Awesome!

My great-granddaughter, Isabelle Mae, was born in May of 2011 to Sheri, the daughter of Johnny and his wife, Sheryl. So I became a Greatgrandmother and Johnny, a Grandfather.

In 2012, I went to Puerto Rico with Gloria and Katie to look at a college there. Lucien and his friend, Nick Battis, came also.

Puerto Rico

Finally, the trip of the century, my fulfillment of my bucket list trip to Paris, France in 2013! This time poor Lucien and Katie pushed me around in a wheelchair that Gloria had purchased, all through France! I had the most wonderful exhilarating moment, meeting MONA LISA face to face! I think I was flying and could not get off the ceiling for days! There was also the palace Versailles and Fountain Chateau with all their glitter and majesty. Also we were able to visit the Rodin museum and view his many sculptures both inside the museum and on the grounds.

In between the above trips I made several trips with Noble Tours of Holton: one to Washington, D.C, another to the Southwest and a trip to New York with Lucien, where we saw a Broadway show. What a little gentlemen Lucien was! I was an envy of the whole group. Another trip that I took with the Noble Tours was when I took my granddaughter, Katie, to Hersheytown, Pennsylvania- CHOCOLATE! she exclaimed! We had fun bonding the two of us that trip! We also saw a wonderful show, Noah, that looked so real! Lastly, somewhere in there, I made a mission trip to Nicaragua with Volunteer in Missions.

So now it is 2015, and I am trying to finish this book of my family and my adventures. Though my health is fairly good, walking has become cumbersome.

My life mostly involves my church with choir, the United Methodist Women, locally and with the Grand Rapid District, my Bible Study group, and volunteering at Vacation Bible School. I enjoy getting together with my church friends, going shopping, dinners at church, the very necessary visits to doctors, my involvement with the local Library Friends, Ladies Aide, various meetings at the church, being an altar steward, and creating banners, etc. I am so thankful that I am still able to drive at the age of eighty-eight, which gives me the opportunity to visit my out of state children and their expanded families. I am also thankful to my daughter for inviting me to travel with her, especially in the later years we have created memories along the life path. My life is still going on despite my age. I guess I do not know WHEN AND HOW TO STOP!

Looking back on my life, there were many joys, but there were also some sorrows along the way. Do I regret some decisions and some events? I certainly do, but without them I would not have been able to appreciate the good that God has given me.

Right now, on the agenda is a trip to Florida to witness the graduation of my grandson, Lucien, from the University of Central Florida. Shortly after, I'll be meeting up with my granddaughter, Katie, in New York City where she is studying art history this summer. Also in New York, I'll be able to visit with my friend, Isabelle, whom I met on one of my trips to Thailand! Still in the planning stages is a trip to Thailand with Gloria and Katie and maybe, just maybe, last visit to my home land Czech Republic? So with God's help, if all this can be accomplished, I say THANK YOU Amen (so be it).

Epilogue

My thoughts on this book ... I realize that by writing this book, my life becomes an open book (that's a pun) and that there will be passages that might be disturbing to some. But these are the facts. To change or erase them is not an option. Life does not always follow the path of our aspirations. I recall a friend who said, "Just because you missed your goal, you do not lose your life." I also feel that God was in charge at all times watching over my family and me even before I really got to know Him.

Still dressing up in the Moravian national costume

So, life does not end, because we lose a goal.